Crossfire

Trapped in the US-Iran Covert War

By

Amir Hekmati

CONTENTS

DEDICATION:1

Forward:2

Prologue:6

    Mansour6

Part One 8

    First Time in Persia8

Chapter One:9

    The Decision 9

Chapter Two 13

    Tehran13

Chapter Three:17

    A Knock on the Door 17

Chapter Four:20

    The Ambush 20

Part Two24

Ward 209...24

Chapter Five: 25

    Evin Prison..25

Chapter Six 29

    Blindfolds and Beatings...29

Chapter Seven: 34

    Sweet Sleep..34

Chapter Eight 37

    Closet American 37

Chapter Nine: 42

    The Barking of the Dog..42

Chapter Ten 48

    Pasdaran Avenue..48

Chapter Eleven: 53

    Scripted and Coerced Confessions.......................................53

Chapter Twelve 60

    Evin, Again...60

Chapter Thirteen 67

    The Judge of Death and The Deceiver.................................67

Chapter Fourteen 76

    Mother...76

Chapter 15: 79

    The Appeal...79

Chapter Sixteen 83

    Rebellion 83

Part Three 90

    Ward 350 90

Chapter Seventeen: 91

    Welcome to Evin University 91

Chapter Eighteen 95

    Mohammad Heydari 95

Chapter Nineteen: 101

    The Electrician 101

Chapter Twenty: 106

    Digital Walk-Ins 106

Chapter Twenty-One: 111

    The Games Played by the Ministry of Intelligence 111

Chapter Twenty-Two: 114

    The Ambassador's Son 114

Chapter Twenty-Three 118

    The Inner Circle 118

Chapter Twenty-Four: 122

    Life on the Outside and the World Inside 122

Chapter Twenty-Five: 126

    Endure 126

Chapter Twenty-Six: 129

Desperation 129

Chapter Twenty-Seven: 132

   Departure 132

Chapter Twenty-Eight: 135

   Family, Again 135

EPILOGUE: 137

DEDICATION:

I dedicate this book to my family who served my prison sentence with me in ways I may never understand.

A special thanks to Congressman Dan Kildee (MI 5th District) who was instrumental in bringing me home, to my fellow Marines who never forgot me, to Montel Williams, a fellow Marine and friend, who fought tirelessly for me, and to the great people of my hometown in Flint, Michigan for their continued support, and to all the people I may never know who voiced their support, thank you.

My release of course would never have been possible without the efforts of the highest levels of the US Government at the time. I'm grateful to President Obama who congratulated my family by phone on the day of my release, to then VP Biden who met with them in person in Michigan, and gave them a tour of Air Force Two, Secretary Kerry who met with me in DC, Brett McGurk who had a direct role in the negotiations, Speaker Ryan and Leader Pelosi who met with me, and helped secure my release, and General Neller- former Commandant of the Marine Corps who met with me on Capitol Hill. My freedom wouldn't have been possible without all of you, and I'm truly grateful, and humbled to be an American.

Forward:

"No comment."

Those were the two words I posted on my personal Facebook timeline in the early morning of January 16, 2016. Just after 5:00 AM, I received a call from Sarah Hekmati, my boss, telling me that her brother, Amir, was finally coming home. For three-and-a-half years, I had added a lot of new contacts on my Facebook page: Marines, domestic and foreign journalists, human rights activists, politicians, television producers, public relations professionals, academics, documentary filmmakers, former hostages, family members of prisoners, and even celebrities. Our common interest was the arrest and unjust imprisonment of Amir Hekmati. On that January morning, rumors quietly began to circulate about the release of five Americans currently imprisoned in Iran. No comment signaled to them not to even ask, because I wouldn't answer. It would be four more hours before CNN interrupted their regular programming to break the story. After the news broke, emails and text messages streamed into my inboxes and phone. Some offered messages of congratulations while others were trying to book Amir's first interview. I was just happy Amir was finally going to be coming home.

I came to work on the campaign to free Amir in 2012. Amir had been in prison in Iran for a year, and his family was working hard for his release, but it was a large task. Amir's sister, Sarah, was working as a guidance counselor, caring for her two young children, and trying to run the campaign on her own. I had been recommended to Sarah by a former client of mine. After an interview, I was soon creating social media accounts, writing statements on behalf of the family, emailing every member of Congress to gain their support and raise awareness about Amir's case, and contacting foreign embassies asking for assistance. As time went on, this was no longer just a job, and the Free Amir campaign wasn't just another client. I became emotionally involved not only in the plight Amir was facing in Iran, but the fight Amir's family was facing in the United States as they advocated for his return. I was in this for the long haul.

Having worked on human rights issues for several years, I knew that Amir's arrest had all the markings of Iranian hostage-taking of political prisoners. Plainclothes intelligence agents would show up at the home of their target, the target would then be taken to a hotel with promises of release after answering a few questions, but from the hotel, they would go to Evin Prison. Once in Evin Prison, they would be held in solitary confinement and interrogated.

Conditions in solitary are intentional. It is easier to solicit a coerced confession from someone at their breaking point. Once their targets have agreed, they would once again go to a hotel. After taking a shower and receiving clean clothes and a meal, recording would begin. Someone from Iran's Ministry of Intelligence and Security would be there to direct the filming. If needed, their target would be forced to record again. They would do this as many times as it took to get it right. These tapes were either edited into documentaries that aired on Iranian state television or used as evidence when they brought in another person for questioning to coerce more cooperation. Instead of being released, as promised, their target would be taken back to Evin Prison.

What was peculiar about Amir's case, however, was that he wasn't just held unjustly in Iran. They took him to court and sentenced him to death. While his death sentence was overturned and a new trial was ordered, that hadn't meant that the death sentence had disappeared, at least from the information we had at the time. And, we didn't have much information, because Amir was still being held in solitary confinement and was not allowed visits or phone calls. While we suspected the overturning of the death sentence meant that Iran had embarrassed itself by acting too hastily, we weren't convinced that his execution wouldn't take place in the middle of the night, and we wouldn't learn about it until the next day. We had a scare in 2013 when I found a post on a Norwegian message board proclaiming Amir had been executed that morning. It wasn't until 2014 that we felt we could breathe a little easier. We learned that Amir had been sentenced to ten years in prison. His conviction went from being an Enemy of God to cooperating with a hostile country.

As time went on – 2012 became 2013, 2013 became 2014, 2014 became 2015, 2015 crept into 2016 – our resolve did not falter. We were determined that Amir would come home. My responsibilities increased as Sarah took the time to help her mother and father, travel to meet with politicians, and did interviews with the media to prevent people from forgetting about Amir.

I was part secretary, part campaign manager, part subject matter expert, part liaison, part researcher, and part decision-maker. Every morning, I scanned Iranian news sites to see if there was any news of Amir, any clues of changes in the political environment, and any sign that this nightmare would soon end not only for Amir but for his family, too. I would help offer perspective. I would try to remain positive. I gave hope where I could. Some nights, though,

Sarah and I cried on the phone together, frustrated because of the injustice of the situation and hurting for Amir and everything he had been put through. My hurt was for Sarah and her family, too. Our hearts were perpetually broken.

When it comes to Amir's imprisonment, I am an expert. For three-and-a-half years, I was in the trenches alongside his family, fighting for his freedom. I know the dates, the times, the places, and the people of his arrest, imprisonment, and release. I can tell you which news networks showed genuine concern for Amir's plight and which networks would air stories only if we managed to come up with an exclusive for them. I can tell you which members of the press asked difficult questions to US officials and which US officials worked on behalf of Amir and which US officials did not. I can tell you about Terry Sharpe, a man who walked from North Carolina to Washington DC wearing a shirt that said Free Amir or Donna in Mississippi and Noel in Missouri that spent several hours a day for four years tweeting about Amir's imprisonment or Nick, a Marine veteran that served with Amir, that went on hunger strike on his behalf or Sean, a professional wrestler that spoke about Amir on podcasts and social media.

What I cannot tell you, though, is Amir's story.

By airing a coerced confession of CIA involvement on Iranian state television, keeping him locked away in solitary confinement, and sentencing him to death, Iran controlled the narrative of Amir's story and took away his voice. This narrative grew in power when, initially,

Amir's family were instructed to remain quiet. In Crossfire: Trapped in the US-Iran Covert War, Amir takes back the narrative and shares his experience in his own words. He tells of the abuse and mistreatment he endured at the hands of Iranian intelligence and the strength, hope, and clarity he found within Evin Prison's walls. He shares the stories of fellow inmates he came to call his friends. It is through his story and theirs that he shares with us a much bigger issue – the covert war between the United States and Iran and the victims it selfishly creates.

Amy Mueller, Campaign Manager

Free Amir Hekmati

Prologue:

Mansour

"They want that guy done, if the hundred go with him f**k 'em." Mansour, an Iranian immigrant, and Texas used car dealer told a member of the Los Zetas Mexican drug cartel as they discussed details of an Iranian intelligence-backed assassination plot. The Iran-Saudi proxy war had been going on for years, but this was a serious escalation. Assassinating the Saudi Ambassador to the United States, Adel al-Jubeir, on US soil in the heart of Washington, D.C., was extremely brazen, even for the Iranians. The cartel member who, unbeknownst to Mansour, was a DEA informant, told Mansour he had scouted the ambassador and a restaurant he frequented in D.C., Café Milano. Mansour told him on orders from an Iranian general he wanted the restaurant bombed when the Ambassador visited and could offer $1.5 million for the hit with a $100k down payment.

With the attack plans allegedly in place, the informant tells Mansour the attack will happen soon, and as a guarantee of completing the payment after the hit, he needed Mansour to travel to Mexico and offer himself as collateral. Mansour agreed and caught a flight to Mexico. He was refused entry by Mexican authorities and sent back to JFK International Airport, where FBI agents awaited to make the arrest. With Mansour in cuffs and the indictment announced, a media frenzy ensues with everyone rushing to the podium to claim credit and announce a successful operation. Robert Mueller, Hillary Clinton, Senators, Congressman, and the Saudi Ambassador all seized the opportunity to not only give thanks to federal agents but also chastise Iran publicly for its reckless behavior. Iran hawks jumped on the opportunity to propose new sanctions, particularly on Iran's Central Banks, and additional punitive measures.

Some doubted the operation, calling it a false-flag, or that it was the actions of a rogue element inside of Iran's Quds Force. A close friend of Mansour's told CNN that if Iran had wanted James Bond, they got themselves Mr. Bean instead, indicating that Mansour was too disorganized and incompetent to execute such an operation. Analysts that were seeking causality for Iran's brazen actions referred to a Wikileaks cable citing diplomatic messages from the Saudi Ambassador to US Officials relaying that the Saudi King had requested the US to attack Iran's then nuclear program characterizing such an attack as "cutting off the head of the snake." Little did I know that Mansour's arrest and the fallout after would affect me in ways I could never imagine.

In August of 2011, I was arrested while visiting my family in Iran. The news an Iranian-backed assassination attempt came about a month later. I believe, at least initially, that his arrest would dictate mine. Phone calls to my family from within Iran during my detention, asking that my family lobby the US government to release Mansour in exchange for my freedom, only confirmed my suspicions. I was a victim of the covert war between the US and Iran. The indirect response from the US Government through intermediaries that my family had engaged in working on my freedom had replied that the US Government would never entertain such a prisoner swap for someone charged with an assassination attempt using explosives. They would be right; as of this writing, Mansour is still in Federal Prison, and I am free to write about it. The four-and-half years I was imprisoned in Iran would take much more from my family and me than our freedom. Many of the impacts are still felt today as we continue to heal from the darkest times of our lives. This is my story. This is the story of the men that I was in prison with that have had their voices silenced or their lights extinguished. Our stories not only tell of the human rights abuses within Iran but explain the longstanding covert war between Iran and the United States of America. We were those caught in the middle. We are their casualties.

Part One

First Time in Persia

Chapter One:
The Decision

I grew up in two worlds. The first world, The United States, is the country I was born to and the country I defended as a United States Marine. The second world I had only experienced through language, meals, family visits, and stories. Iran. My parents' homeland. My grandmother, Badri, visited the United States each year, speaking with us in Farsi – a language I learned as a young boy, cooking us traditional Persian dishes, and sharing stories of her life in Iran. Although I grew up hearing the stories and speaking the language, it was a country that was still a mystery to me. A land of misconception. A land of culture. A land of history. A land of natural beauty. Home.

As my flight was about to take off in Dubai, I sent an email to my mother telling her how excited I was for my first trip to Iran. I was excited to see the grandmother that influenced so much of my young life. I had a long list of uncles, aunts, and cousins I would be visiting. I had never seen any of them in person. While we knew one another, this would be our first chance to look at one another face-to-face and embrace. A month earlier, my mother, sister, and younger brother had visited those same family members in Iran. They have visited several times. What made their last visit so important and inspired my travels was the news that my grandmother was very ill and might not have much time left in this world. I needed to see her one last time. If it were not for this news, my trip to Iran might never have happened.

Although I was always intrigued by Iran and wanted to know my relatives more closely, my life was busy. With the conflict on-going between the US and Iran, I had concerns. My biggest concern was the interpretation of Iran's laws regarding citizenship. At the time, Iran's citizenship laws applied to blood, specifically the blood of the father, and since my father was born in Iran and Iran did not recognize dual citizenship, Iran's citizenship laws interpreted me as an Iranian citizen even though I had never set foot in that country and was born in the US. With Iranian citizenship came compulsory military service. There was always a chance that if I traveled there, I might not be permitted to leave until I served a 24-month tour in the Iranian army.

With so many Iranians living outside of the country, Iran realized that the compulsory military law was outdated and began issuing three-month travel visas for Iranians wishing to travel to their country. I was still hesitant, though, so I contacted a DC-based Iranian-American lawyer who confirmed this with the Iranian consulate inside the embassy of Pakistan. The consulate replied through my lawyer that I'd need to apply for an Iranian passport to enter the country. I didn't know if this was going to be a problem because I formally renounced my Iranian citizenship when I enlisted in the US Marines in 2001. The Department of Defense (DOD) didn't allow dual nationality for certain countries, and I sent a notarized letter to the Iranian consulate in DC on DOD letterhead renouncing all ties to the government of Iran. The letter was to make it clear that I was in no way Iranian. The DOD sent the letter on my behalf via certified mail.

I consulted with my lawyer about the letter sent by DOD, and his advice was that if they're still demanding to issue me a passport, and I traveled there as an Iranian citizen, there is no reason for scrutiny. I hesitantly took his advice and proceeded with the visa application. After all, my mother, brother, and sister had just been in Iran, stated all was calm, and my relatives there were not political people. The lawyer mentioned to me that 2 million Iranian Americans visit regularly. He told me that he had processed many visas and passports for Iranian-Americans in various US government positions, and there has never been an issue. I trusted his experience and expertise on the matter.

I had read about the three American hikers that had been arrested for crossing the Iranian border, but where they traveled to, and the circumstances of their arrest were completely different from my travel plans. I knew of the detention of some journalists, but I didn't have a past as a journalist, and the political situation in Iran was different now than it was at the time of their arrest two years earlier. I remembered reading about a US soldier who somehow got re-routed to Tehran instead of Kabul on a flight from the USA. The soldier arrived at Imam Khomeini airport wearing his US Military uniform! Besides being frowned upon by Iranian airport officials, he was re-routed on another flight from Tehran to Kabul with no issue. I also thought about all the American journalists stationed in

Tehran, reporting routinely on Iran and American issues, and freely traveling back and forth. The State Department had only issued a level two "Exercise Increased Caution" travel advisory; the same travel advisory Mexico had in 2011. Nothing in the literature said "Do Not Travel" as it does now.

I would be entering on an Iranian passport and visiting family who had lived there their entire lives. With the reassurances of my lawyer and my family's recent visit and the knowledge that my grandmother's health was failing and failing fast, I knew this was a trip that I needed to make, and if I didn't make it now, I would probably not get the opportunity to go again.

"It's his fault. Why did he go to Iran?"

"What did he expect going to Iran when he has served in the US military?" "Who goes to Iran for a vacation anyway? It's IRAN."

The comment section of articles spanning the first days of imprisonment where I was interrogated and tortured to my return home was littered with these opinions. I would think that these comments come mostly from people who have no family in or interest in traveling to Iran in the first place. They have had the good fortune of having their relatives apart from their lives in their home states or home countries their whole lives. They have had the joy of celebrating holidays together. When tragedy strikes, they have had the benefit of surviving it together. The idea of having to travel to another country to hug your uncle for the first time or have a meal with your cousin or say goodbye to your grandmother is foreign to them.

I longed to visit the grandmother that had traveled thousands of miles to visit me and meet the family I knew only from letters, phone calls, and pictures. I wanted to see the homes that my father and mother grew up in and walk the streets they walked in their youth. I wanted to eat authentic Persian food and shop in Persian stores. I wanted to meet the people that helped shape who my parents are and, in turn, helped shape me.

The reasons for my imprisonment were in response to events that had nothing to do with me. I wasn't held hostage because of my profile or my background. Higher profile Iranian-Americans that have worked for the government or are wealthy businessmen would have been targeted if this were the case. I was a victim in the covert war between Iran and the United States that balances on sanctions, intelligence, imprisonment of dual citizens, and at the time, a nuclear agreement between Iran and the rest of the world. I was a convenient target. One that Iran didn't think anyone would miss. They were wrong.

Chapter Two
Tehran

After a short flight from Dubai to Tehran aboard Emirates Airlines, I landed at the not so spectacular Imam Khomeini International. Heading into customs with my new Iranian passport, I was waved over by a heavily-bearded, overweight customs agent. I watched the agent as he rarely looked up, asked a few questions, scanned passports, and sent other passengers on their way. When I approached, he stuck his hand out for the passport, scanned, and paused for a second.

"Where did you get your passport?" "America," I replied.

He looked up for the first time and made slight eye-contact with me. After another pause, he handed me back my passport and called the next person in line. This was the part that made me the most nervous. That was easy! After his dismissal, I went to gather my luggage. With my luggage in hand, I headed for the doors to grab a taxi. As I neared the door, an older man wearing a loose-fitting suit and a tired, serious look on his face walked towards me and pointed to an office. Confused, I asked him what he meant, and he said, "Please, Inspection" in Farsi. No ID, no uniform, just a guy in a suit, waiting for me to almost exit the airport before sending me to the inspection area. I was getting nervous. I asked a few questions, but he just kept pointing to the inspection area. My intuition told me that arguing with this guy or just walking off wouldn't end well, so I followed his instructions.

After a brief luggage scan, I was handed off to another agent who went through my things. Later, in Evin Prison, cellmates would tell me that the luggage scanners can grab information off laptops, and cellphones and that a tracking device would be placed in the luggage to track you during your trip.

"I think you are a good person," the man said to me after inspecting my things.

How strange.

He told me to pack up, so that's what I did. As I headed for the exit, I could feel him staring at me. His stare made me move quicker. Finally, in the taxi, I made my way to my uncle's house. The ride to my uncle's house was my first taste of Tehran, and I was in awe of what I saw. The mountains surrounding Tehran were beautiful. The traffic in Tehran was overwhelming. The Iranians I saw as I peered out my taxi window were young, and everyone seemed in a hurry. Tehran was a young city.

We approached my uncle's neighborhood, an upscale area formerly called Jordan, now officially known as Nelson Mandela Boulevard. My uncle was a wealthy real estate developer with interests in oil and gas. The homes in his neighborhood rivaled some of the finest homes I had seen in America. Most people without a connection to Iran think that Iran is a run-down country, and Tehran is a run-down city full of poor and uneducated people. Those are the images shown most in the West, along with groups of people chanting "Death to America." The reality is that it is like any other society. There is poverty. There is also opulence and wealth.

My cousin, Anousheh, knew I was arriving and met me at the door with a huge smile, a big hug, and welcomed me into my uncle's sprawling home. My uncle was sipping tea in the walled-off backyard by the pool and walked over to greet me. This was the first time I had held either of these people, my family, in my arms. My uncle and I sat together in the living room and talked while Anousheh brought in wave after wave of snacks, Persian sweets, and tea as is customary in most Persian homes. I felt right at home. I was happy to discover this family of mine but also upset that I had been deprived of them my whole life. I wished I had visited sooner.

The Shah was in power when my father married my mother in Tehran. They traveled to the US for my father's education. He was working on his PH.D. War broke out while my father was finishing his studies. The Iran-Iraq war carried on for eight long years. During that time, my mother was pregnant with my older sister. My twin sister and I would soon follow. My parents decided that any parent would – to stay in the US and raise us. My father, a brilliant scientist, had no shortage of work opportunities, and we called Flagstaff, Arizona, home before finding our way to Michigan. We were safe in the US and had a great life, but that great life came at a cost.

We had no relatives. We just had each other. It is a loneliness that a lot of first and second-generation Americans know too well.

For the first time in Iran, I was able to know what it meant to be a part of an extended family. I was able to receive wisdom from an uncle, companionship from a cousin, and unconditional love from an aunt. Any anxiety I had about my trip to Iran had completely left my mind. With my family, I felt right at home.

After an abundance of sweets, snacks, and tea, Anousheh drove me to see my grandmother. My grandmother lived in an area called Pars. We drove up to the four-story home where my grandmother occupied the top two floors with her maid. My aunt occupied the second floor, and my grandmother rented the first floor to a tenant. My grandfather owned a large glass factory in Tehran. I had heard many great stories about him and his life. He passed from prostate cancer years before, and I hoped to put flowers on his grave. It would be my first time meeting him.

Anousheh buzzed the door.

"Yes?" my grandmother's maid answered.

"It's me, and I have a guest. Is Grandma awake?" said into the speaker

I could hear my grandma tell Anousheh to come in, and the buzzer went off. We entered, went to the elevator, and carried us to my grandmother's door. The maid had left the door open.

"Hi Grandma, I have a present for you," Anousheh said as she waved at me to walk in.

With a big smile on my face, I walked in and waved at my grandma. She burst into tears and called me over for a hug. After a long embrace, one I had waited for years to have, we sat together, and I told her how happy I was to be with her. She was ecstatic. She couldn't stop smiling. Despite all of the trouble I had to go through to make this trip happen, it was worth it to see her this happy, full of life, and energy. She was able to forget about being sick while we laughed and talked for hours. Grandma told me stories of me as a young child, my uncles, and my late grandfather. She told me how much she missed me.

The next three weeks in Tehran would be some of the greatest memories of my life.

Almost every day, I received invitations to see uncles and cousins. We had family gatherings and dinners together. I was amazed to see how many relatives I had that I had never met and was humbled by how they welcomed me into their homes and the happiness they had from meeting me. I visited a famous bazaar, Darakeh - a popular spot near a scenic stream atop a mountain, and Lavasun - a scenic area where my uncles' own a cabin overlooking the valleys beneath. Natural beauty surrounds Tehran. It is a great city filled with culture and history. Three weeks was not enough time to explore everything there was to see in Tehran. Only a few days of my stay left, I was dreading leaving. I had only begun to get to know my many relatives, and there was so much left undone. With only a 90-day limit on my visa, and classes starting for me soon at the University of Michigan, it was time to go home.

Chapter Three:
A Knock on the Door

It was just after 11:00 AM on August 29, 2011. It had rained the night before. I was staying at a second apartment my Uncle owned in the Farmaniya neighborhood my family had arranged for me for my stay while in Iran. I had just finished a late breakfast and decided to drink some tea, and watch the news. I was startled by a knock on the door. Since no visitors were expected that day, I went to the door and looked at the security camera monitor on the buzzer phone common in Iran, and saw no one. I opened the door to check the hallway, and from around the corner – outside of camera view came three men. Without showing ID, they asked to come into the house, but this was not a request. This was a demand. As they step into the home, they are courteous but firm. Two men stand by the doorway, earpieces on, and the side of their suits bulging out. They are the muscle. The third man, slightly older, started pacing the home and making small talk. I notice the two men at the door surveilling the home.

As the man paces, he asks about pictures on the wall, and asks my name. He pretends not to know who I am. He asks where I'm from, and I respond by saying I'm visiting from the United States.

"America?" he says.

"Welcome to Iran," he says.

"What brings you here?" he asks. "Visiting my family," I say.

"Very good," he says.

"Is everything going okay?" he asks. "So far so good," I responded.

"Mr. Hekmati," he responds, "We need to ask a few questions about your passport. You need you to come with us for a little while. You should be back very quickly."

I'm sitting at the table as the man looks me in the eye. His hands are in his pocket. He glances over to the two, heavyset men by the door, glances back at me, and then leaves the house. The two men by the door ask me to follow them. They say this in a way that we all know that this is not optional. I must go. I reluctantly agreed, and left the house with one of the two men at each of my sides and walked towards two waiting Samands -an Iranian made automobile. Both cars are running with drivers waiting to escort us to our next destination. They guided me into the vehicle with blacked-out windows. I sit in the backseat of the vehicle with one man sitting on my left and one on my right. Considering how small the vehicle is, this was a snug fit, making it almost impossible to jump out of the car or run. Both thoughts crossed my mind.

As we zip through Tehran's streets with heavy traffic, the driver takes all kinds of shortcuts and somehow seems to glide through the maze of traffic that is Tehran's streets. Something you'll often hear in Tehran is that if you can drive there, you can drive anywhere. This guy was definitely a professional. My two escorts glance over, offering a few controlled smiles.

"You were in the military?" one of them asks. "Yes," I respond, "US Military, four years."

"Did you ever go to Iraq? Or Afghanistan?" "Iraq," I say.

"Karbala, Najaf?" He asks about these Iraqi cities because they have majority Shi'ite populations and are the home of Shi'ite holy shrines. Iran is distinguished from other countries in the region because they are a Shi'ite Muslim country, sometimes called Shia, where other countries hold Sunni populations.

"No," I respond, "I was in Ramadi in the Anbar province." They stare at me.

"How much were you paid? As US Military?" one asks. I noticed that this was of extreme interest to them.

"Around $2000.00 per month."

"How much is that in our money?" they both asked. "About 3.5 million tomans," I tell them.

They both stare intently at me, trying to digest what I just said and then both look away and out the window and then back at me. Both men are annoyed by my answer.

"3.5 million! That's a lot of money!" one says.

I asked how much they made. I found out that it amounted to about 1 million tomans a month. At the time, that was roughly $800 US dollars. These were mid level intelligence officers in their mid-thirties. It frustrated them to know that an 18-year-old, voluntary

American Service member with the rank of Sergeant was making almost four times what they were.

Chapter Four:
The Ambush

We finally pulled up to our destination, an all white, windowless two story building with soldiers standing in front in camo fatigues carrying AK-47's. The agents parked, we stepped out and began walking towards the lobby. One agent was in front of me, and one was behind me in a staggered fashion. We headed to the main doors, and the agent hit the intercom button, a buzz was heard and we walked past metal detectors. I was escorted to an all white room that was mostly empty with a small desk, and chair. I was faced towards the wall, the guards told me to wait there, and left the room.

A few minutes later, there was a slight knock on the door, and the guards moved to open it. I couldn't see any of this, but I could hear it. I heard footsteps and whispers; they were directly to my left. I was still confused, a little anxious, but started to get irritated that I had been in a corner facing the wall like a child. I could hear two more chairs placed in position behind me. I can sense two people sitting behind me, whispering to each other. "Haji" speaks, this will be a voice that will be my only contact for the next 18 months.

"Mr. Amir, how are you?" he asked.

"Fine," I say, "Can I ask what this is about?"

"Why don't you tell us," he said with a firm voice.

"I don't know what you mean," I said as I grew frustrated with this game Haji was playing.

"Amir, we know everything. We are a global intelligence service; we've been watching you for a long time. We know where you live, your family, and your friends. You need to be honest with us. If you are, then nothing will happen. You'll walk out of here. Otherwise, things will go very bad for you," he threatened me.

"I have no idea what you are talking about. I was told I'd be coming to talk about my passport."

"I'm going to leave the room and give you one minute to think about what decision you want to make. Be honest, say everything. Right now, you are in a nice place. Your relatives are waiting for you. You don't want that to go away, do you?" "Why don't you tell me what you're talking about," I replied.

"You know what we're talking about," he said, "60 seconds starting now."

I felt an immediate rush of panic that seemed to start in my gut and slowly expand up to my heart and lungs. My heart rate went up, and my breathing grew heavy. I was speechless. I didn't know what to say, so I said nothing. I heard his footsteps heading toward the door, exaggerating for effect. He was bluffing. He had to be. The door opened slowly, and I stayed silent. My 60 seconds were up.

Haji stepped in and asked if I remember anything. I replied no.

"You made a very big mistake," he said. It sounded like he was making his way outside the doorway.

The door closed. I sensed the two agents that brought me here standing behind me. One told me to stand up, and I reluctantly obeyed orders. I looked around the room and saw it was now only me and my two escorts. Everyone had gone. There was an eerie feeling of loneliness and dread that came over me. For three weeks, everything was going well. I was with my relatives. I was enjoying my life. Here I was, in a foreign country, in a weird room, surrounded by agents, facing walls, and talking to some mystery man that I wasn't allowed to look in the eye.

My emotions began to move between panic and anger. One part of me wanted to shout at them and ask what the hell was going on and another part of me felt that I should wait until we are in the lobby and out of this quiet room where a bullet could easily be put through my head, and no one would know.

We walked out of the room, and I looked back to get one last glance at the room. I'm trying to memorize all the details that I can. There was an eeriness at that moment that I'll never forget.

The demeanor of the two guards was no longer friendly, but cold and serious. Grim. At this point, I don't know what my fate will be, but two agents are standing to my left and right, and I feel choked.

At this moment, I knew that I would not be making any decisions on my own. I felt like I was choking. Two invisible hands were wringing the life out of me as we walked outside the building to a van with blacked-out windows waiting for me. It became obvious that preparations were already in place for me should I not cooperate with Haji.

I entered the van with tinted windows and placed in the back seat. One agent sat in the second row of seats blocking the van's sliding door. The other agent took his position in the passenger seat next to the driver. Restraints were locked firmly around both my index fingers.

They were extremely tight, and any swift movement of my hands would break my fingers. We departed the hotel and zipped through Tehran's traffic. At this point, I had no idea where I was in the city. I broke the silence and asked the agent where they were taking me.

"Somewhere good," he responded.

His answer made me more nervous. I looked around, trying desperately to get an idea of where I was as different scenarios ran through my head.

"Where the hell are you taking me?" I asked again, this time, angrier. "Have I committed a crime? Why the hell do I even have to go along with this!"

"Just relax. We are just following orders. When we get to where we're going, you can talk to Haji," he said as he dismissed me and my anger.

"Haji? Who the hell is Haji? I only know his voice! I was facing a wall." "Just relax," he told me again, "We'll be there soon."

I looked through the windows for clues, and then my questions were answered. Outside my window in front and on the right hung a sign that read "Evin Prison." The agent pulls a blindfold out of his coat pocket and hands it to me and tells me to put it on.

The light is gone; my world went dark.

Part Two
Ward 209

Chapter Five:
Evin Prison

With the blindfold on, I heard the van pulling through what sounded like a checkpoint. The agents in the van and the guards working the entrance exchanged words. The smell from the van's exhaust crept in through the open window of the van. My heart rate increased. I felt like I was being punched in the guts. I began to feel light-headed. We had entered Evin Prison's vast prison complex.

We drove up what felt like a hill and turned a corner. The sliding door opened, and the guard told me to come as he reached his hand out for mine. I g see my feet and the feet of the agent escorting me. Being blindfolded has an instant effect on you. It amplifies your fears because you are disoriented. It humiliates you because you need help doing even the simplest of tasks. It also makes it difficult for you to resist or escape. Being at a notorious prison in a foreign country tilted my imagination. Those in charge that I couldn't see took on the role of monsters in my mind. For some of them, this wasn't far from the truth.

With the blindfold still on, the agent escorting me guided me by my arm to a small, dirty room that looked like a storage facility. He sat me down in an old wooden chair. Walking with the blindfold on had been so jarring that it was a relief to be stationary. Through the bottom of the blindfold, I could see feet moving around me and heard chatter in the distance. Another man came and asked me to stand. I was able to remove my blindfold. He handed me a bag and told me to strip down to my underwear and put my personal belongings in the cloth sack in front of me.

"I want to call the Swiss Embassy," I informed him.

"There is no embassy. There is no lawyer. Just do what I ask, or we will ask you in a different way."

"I'm not doing anything. You can do whatever you want, but I need to call my family or someone to let them know I'm here."

An immediate silence fell over the room. I tilted my head up to see that the door was open, and the man was gone. I was alone, not knowing what would happen next. Thirty seconds later, I heard heavy footsteps approaching. Two bulky men with batons in their hand entered and walked towards me. One immediately landed a blow from a baton on my left thigh while the other struck at my rib cage. It was hard enough that it induced pain, but luckily not hard enough to crack my rib. The baton strikes continued to land, sending instant pain throughout the body. The blindfold added to the anxiety of anticipating further blows. I tried to step out of the way of the batons, turning sideways to shield my ribs and using my arms. I tore off the blindfold and took a defensive posture backing up away from the batons. With no blindfold on, I could see the two men staring at me with their batons ready to strike again.

"I don't know why I am here. I have not been charged with anything! What do you want from me?" I shouted at them.

Two more guards dressed in military uniforms rushed in and pulled out handcuffs. A third guard, an older man, stood behind them and ordered them to put the cuffs on me. The two guards in military uniforms approached me. They outnumbered me. I reluctantly held out my hands, and the cuffs locked around my wrists. One guard handed me my prison uniform- light blue cotton pajamas. I put my feet into them one at a time. They threw a shirt over my shoulder, and the blindfold was once again put over my eyes. The guards escorted me into another van.

The pain from the baton strikes was starting to abate, but I could tell that there was going to be some swelling. I could feel it happening already.

The van drove uphill for about 5 minutes until it stopped, and we moved out. The guards guided me by the arm. The handcuffs were still on, and we climbed up three flights of stairs. On my feet are cheap sandals with no socks. We moved up to the top of the steps to a heavy, old, rusted steel door that opened slowly and walked in. Here I was handed off to two men wearing the signature button-up shirt and trousers that most Iranian intelligence agents wear. We walked into the hallway of the cell block. The prison looked like something from a horror movie. The concrete floor was wet, recently hosed down, and splashes of water hit my bare feet as I walked. The light flickered on and off. On each side of me were doors that looked like the tops of caskets. Behind each door was a life held in limbo. There was banging on the doors, and people were crying out - cries of agony and cries of desperation. The cold, heartless guards are unmoved by this as they hurriedly escort me to my cell. I wasn't human to them, but an item they were going to place into storage.

The guards swung the door open, and I looked up to find a small enclosed cell waiting for me. The floor was concrete. There was a small, tin toilet that smelled horrible and a filthy sink with a used bar of soap. I reluctantly walk in and immediately reach the end of it. This cell was three feet by five feet with very thick walls and no windows. A casket indeed. I walked in, and the extremely bright light blinded me. The door slammed behind me.

Everything was stale- there was no air getting in or out. I felt the pressure in the room increase. Sound disappeared. It felt like the weight of the prison walls was pushing down on me.

I found a place in the corner and sat down to regroup. I was a 27-year-old man with plans for my life. I was motivated. I was athletic. I was full of ambition and hopeful about my future. I was to start my education soon. I looked at my feet. Barefoot. I looked at my clothes— the humiliating uniform of a prisoner. I looked at my hands, still cuffed. I had spent my morning at my uncle's lush home, and now I was sitting on the concrete floor of a prison cell in Iran. My brain had a difficult time processing the contradictions. I began to lose my thoughts.

My emotions teetered between despair and sadness. I leaned my head against the cold cell wall. As my eyes grew heavy, I prayed this was a bad dream, and I would wake up to see my family.

Chapter Six

Blindfolds and Beatings

I woke in a complete daze. I forget where I am for a moment. When I remember, I need to take deep breaths to get my bearings. A few moments of sheer terror passed, and I started to feel like I was slowly being stabbed. I would feel this feeling every day of my life for the next five years. It was the horror of waking up to this place. There was a saying in prison: "We die every day, each minute is a thousand minutes, each day is a thousand days." I was getting my first taste of this. I tried calming myself, "Shake it off" You need to relax. We will get this sorted out. My breathing was constricted, and I started to wonder if there was something wrong with the air because I could not breathe.

I went to the sink filled with soap stains, hair, and the grime of I don't even know what. I turn on the water and what comes out is brownish-gold, and I step back in disgust. Once the water comes out clear, I hesitate. Maybe water would refresh me and make me feel alive. I held my hands to catch some and splashed my face. I began pacing back and forth a bit more. I don't know what time it is. I don't know how long I have been sleeping. The handcuffs are still around my wrists. I started to panic. Then I started to get angry, and I begin to shout.

"Why am I here?"

"This is bullshit!"

My temper grew as my voice rose. I put all my energy into the sole of my food as I drive it into the door. BAM! I do it again. BAM! As I get ready to launch my foot into the door for the third time, I hear hammering on the wall next to me — Thump, thump, thump. There is someone there! I'm next to a living thing, another prisoner, and he likes my rebellion. BAM! A third kick into the door. BAM! A fourth. I heard some distant grunts and yells and can tell some are fellow prisoners, and some are startled guards. Just the fifth kick is loaded and ready to be propelled into the door when the small hatch in the door opens, and an angry face wearing a face mask regards me with contempt. His eyes are crazed, and his beard is protruding out of the sides of his surgical mask. Guards wear these masks to hide their identities. He continues to stare me down.

"Someone want to tell me what I'm doing here?" I say to him.

He stares a moment longer and slams the hatch shut, not saying a word. I hit the release button on that 5th kick in the door. My sheer rage is connecting bone and muscle to steel, and I'm making noise. I can hear the other prisoners getting riled up in support. I feel satisfaction from this. I feel like I'm not alone. Others are here with me. We are suffering together.

Moments later, the door flew open. There are three guards with batons in their hands. I'm defenseless, still in handcuffs, and back myself against the very thick wall that contains me in this small cage. It's obvious that they have a huge advantage, and I won't be able to put up much of a fight, so I brace myself. They march into my small cell, yelling at me about kicking the door. One grabbed the chain in between my hands on the handcuff while the other jabs the baton into my ribs. I know that any major resistance will be answered with more powerful baton strikes, so I do my best to push them away and keep a distance where I can block the blows. My handcuffs are pulled up by one guard to a plumbing pipe in the ceiling, and another guard uses his handcuffs to chain me to the pipe. A few more batons landed on my rib area and legs leaving me bruised. The guards leave. Everything is silent again.

I'm in an extremely uncomfortable position. My feet are planted on the ground, but my hands are elevated. My wrists are under lots of pressure, and I can feel my hands going to sleep. I'm starving, tired, and still in disbelief of the situation. I have no idea what time it is and think of my parents and my relatives. They don't know where I am. I know that they are worried. Later on, I would learn that my family came to Evin Prison five times only to be told I wasn't there.

The sixth time they paid a bribe to a prison official, and my whereabouts were made known to them. I wasn't only in the notorious Evin Prison, but I was in the notorious Ward 209, a prison within a prison run by Iran's Ministry of Intelligence.

I begin to obsess about my hands. I'm worried my arms will separate from my body or that my wrists will no longer function. I call out to the guards several times an hour, but no one comes. I'm so tired and hungry. Starving. My legs throbbed from the baton blows. My ribs do, too. I want to go home. I begin to scold myself. Why didn't I just stay home? Only one day has passed in Ward 209.

"Are you going to calm down now? Finished?" a guard asked me hours later.

The guard removes the handcuffs, and I can finally bring my hands down. I massage them for the next forty minutes. Great relief comes when the blood starts flowing in them again.

A dinner cart finally comes by and brings me lentils, hot tea, and stale bread. My body was in crisis most from the physical and psychological stress, and I hadn't eaten anything in forty-eight hours. Today, just thinking of lentils makes me nauseous, but it tasted like filet mignon to me that night. Sugar cubes are given with the potent tea, and I add as many as I can. The tea comes in thin plastic cups that would melt if you didn't drink it fast enough.

As soon as I finish eating, I rest my head and fell into a deep sleep. It is the first night I dreamt the dream that I would have many times through my imprisonment. In the dream, I'm free. I'm walking around an outdoor mall somewhere in the USA. The weather, the sun, and palm trees are putting a smile on my face, and I don't have a care in the world. I pass a point in the mall, and the shops, people, and attire of the people start to become like that of Iran. The modern shops turn into Tehran streets. The store facades faded. English on the store windows turned into Farsi, and the employees transformed into bearded men with toothpicks or cigarettes in their mouths. The spotless walkways transform into the open sewers. The laughing, happy faces of Americans walking in the mall changed into headscarves and bearded men with serious faces and exhaustion in their eyes.

I walk with astonishment as this transformation happens. In my dream a horrible feeling overcomes me as I realize that I'm not free. In my dream I had been imprisoned in Iran, but had made it back to the US. Somehow I ended up back in Iran after vowing never to go back again.

Slowly after the transformation happens, I'm arrested again and taken back to Evin Prison. This dream would reoccur in various forms during my imprisonment. After I gained my freedom, this dream would continue to haunt me. I would wake up with dread and then instantly feel relief after I realized I was home and free and not in Iran.

****

"Let's go! Your interrogator is here," the guard growled at me as he woke me. I was slow to get up and hesitant about being questioned again. On the one hand, Haji held the keys to my freedom. On the other, being interrogated was always a stressful experience. I dreaded hearing again that they would keep me in solitary confinement to rot away. The tiny cell, the bright lights on 24 hours a day, the floor, these ridiculous prison pajamas, the stench of the toilet in the cell. All of this was starting to take its toll on me. My mind was beginning to turn against me, too, and I was not only a prisoner to my cell but a prisoner to my mind.

From my cell, I'm led to the interrogation room. I was sat in a chair and kept waiting. I would hear the whispers and know that it was time to begin this all over again. There were always two interrogators, Haji and a mystery man. They played good cop and bad cop. Haji, though, was the man in charge.

"Is it going well?" Haji would ask. The sarcasm and indifference in his voice were meant to anger me.

"It's not bad," I'd reply.

"Did you remember anything?" "No," I would answer.

"We're getting tired of coming here. Next time, we'll leave for six months or more before coming back. If we come back."

"In six months, I still won't know what it is you want or what I'm supposed to say." I heard papers shuffling and footsteps coming towards me.

"You made a mistake," Haji says as he taps my shoulder.

And then silence. I'm left alone in the interrogation room. Haji's talk of six months crept into my mind. Rationally, I knew it was a threat meant to make me talk, but as I sat in the interrogation room alone, I pictured my hair turning gray in Evin Prison. Haji would say, "We'll leave you here until your hair is as white as your teeth."

"Get up!" a guard shouted at me.

My blindfold returns to my face and I walk the dreadful walk back to my cell. The door closed, and I could feel something inside my soul breaking. This time was different. This wasn't a bluff. God knows when, or if, Haji would come back. I felt as though I'd lost my opportunity.

The desperation would begin to kick in. I began questioning myself. Had I not told him everything? Is there something I am forgetting? Am I bringing this all on myself? I would comb over every detail of my life until Haji would come again.

Chapter Seven:
Sweet Sleep

I began to disconnect from myself. The desperation and misery made me feel like I was no longer human. Any thought or memory about my days as a free man only caused me more pain and made my imprisonment harder. Ironically, the best aspects of my life turned to daggers in my brain, and haunted me every minute of every day as each thought reminded me of what was being stolen from me. Thoughts of family, freedom, nature, and all the things that would normally bring a smile to my face, brought me anxiety, and sadness instead. I looked at those memories with fear, and sadly tried to avoid the thought of them. I didn't want to be reminded of what was being taken away from me. I wanted to imagine that I was born in this cell, and this was all I knew.

Mealtime became my clock. It was the only time I could see another person, hear outside noise, see the door open. The sight of that door opening gave me a glimpse of the outside world because my world was now this 1.5-meter by t3-meter cell. Seeing the outside world gave me hope. As soon as the door shut, the hope would leave me.

Over the next few months, days came and went in blurs. Some days, my mind would wander when I woke up, and a whole day would pass with me lost in my thoughts. Other days I was filled with so much anxiety and depression that I felt like I was suffocating. On these days, those panic-filled days, I'd bang on the door, turn on my light for the guard to come every five minutes, argue with them about why I was there, and pace as much as I could in the room I was restricted to while thinking of ways I could escape. The merciless walls of solitary change the people they house, making them just as merciless.

I grew angrier the longer I was locked up alone. I couldn't come to terms with the fact that those responsible for imprisoning me and mistreating me could wander around freely, enjoy dinner with their families, and sleep easy at night while I was rotting away for no reason at all and the lives of my family were in upheaval. I began to imagine ways to get my revenge against the guards, interrogators, and anyone who resembled it. I lost the part of my heart that could and often did forgive anything. I knew that the forgiving part of me was being replaced with something else, and I feared that would remain with me even after I left this God-forsaken place. At times these feelings of rage felt like empowerment. Other times, they felt like poison.

I began to wither away and lose weight. The lack of angles in the room would make it seem like the room was closing in on me. That would cause panic attacks. The bright light was kept on 24-hours a day to induce sensory deprivation. The lack of sleep made me talk to myself. I had conversations with people that were not there. Sleep would find me once I had exhausted myself. I woke up from that slumber immediately filled with anxiety again. And the process would start all over the next day. Day in, day out.

I WILL NO LONGER BE HERE! I screamed in my mind. As if it was simply a matter of will. If I willed it strongly enough, the doors would fly open, and freedom would be mine. I replayed scenes from the action movies I watched at home in the US in my mind. The scenes where the actors had all the odds stacked against them and, in a last-ditch effort, defeats his enemies and is victorious. I pounded the door for the guard. Eventually, usually after a few hours, an angry guard would ask me what the hell I wanted in Farsi. I would unleash my anger on them. My anger erased the memory of batons and stressed positions I had previously endured.

I threatened a hunger strike, hurled insults at my interrogators, and called this place "Evintanamo" - a reference to Guantanamo, a popular tool used by Iran to justify mistreatment of inmates - to their faces, and I would throw my food on the ground outside my cell through the food slot in the door.

On a particularly bad day, I waited for the batons to come or for them to meek out some other twisted punishment they had in store for me. To my surprise, guards with batons didn't open my door, but a doctor did. He wore a surgical mask with a white lab coat. Unlike the guards that kept their surgical masks on to hide their identities, and maybe their shame, he pulled down his mask and spoke with me calmly. He explained that he was a doctor that specializes in anxiety and that even though he couldn't help me with my case or intervene with my interrogator, he could give me something to calm me down. He handed me a cup with three or four pills. He told me to swallow them in front of him and that they would make me sleep. While my goal was to annoy the guards into submission, the thought of simply swallowing a few pills and escaping this hell for a little while sounded achievable. I could riot another day.

Today, I would choose to sleep. I took the pills with a quick gulp of water. The doctor left, and my cell door closed. I sat in the corner of the cell and felt my eyelids get heavy. It felt like invisible hands were tucking me into bed like I was a child. For the first time since my imprisonment, I would sleep – really sleep.

After waking the next morning, I felt so much better. It made me realize just how much damage had been done to me. My brain had been in crisis mode for a long time and was thanking me for being able to shut down for a night. The pill's effect would continue all day, making me feel lethargic and unbothered. I just sat in the corner of the cell, dazed, staring at the walls for hours. Time passed, and that was a good thing. I knew that at the end of the day, I would sleep and get to escape this reality again for a few hours. That was also a good thing. Twice a day, someone in a surgical mask and a white lab coat would deliver that little cup with a few colorful pills that would help me cope. I looked forward to the twice-daily visits from the doctor. Not only did he offer me salvation in pill form, he provided me with contact with someone from out there, the out there I longed to return to soon.

Chapter Eight

Closet American

In the middle of my morning breakfast of stale bread, butter, and marmalade, the door swung open. The guard told me to get up and put my blindfold on because my interrogator wanted to see me. By this time, I was familiar with the path to my interrogation room. I was familiar with the sounds of the guards leaving the room. I was familiar with the shuffle of two pairs of feet entering. I was familiar with the change in the air when he entered the room. I was familiar with his good cop and bad cop routine with another man I would never know.

"All you do is lie, lie, lie, Amir. We both know why you came here, so why don't you just tell us!" Haji opened, sounding flustered.

"Listen, Haji, or whatever your name is, I don't know what you're talking about. I just came here to see my family. You keep telling me that I know. Know what?!"

"You tell us, Amir! We already know. We want you to tell us. Be honest, and we'll help you. You can go home, and this will all be over. If you don't, well, we have ways to make you talk. I will ask you in a different way next time," he threatened me.

"Please just tell me what you're talking about? There has to be a misunderstanding."

"I'm sorry, Amir. That was your last chance. You blew it! You messed up again, and life is going to be very hard for you. You're going to stay here until your hair becomes as white as your teeth. It's too late now. Even if you want to tell me the truth now, I won't hear it."

"What are you talking about? This is crazy! I thought this was a religious country. You've talked to me about God, and you're always talking about God here. So, what about God?" It was me who was growing frustrated now.

Haji chuckles, "God?! In here, I am God."

I heard him get up. I heard his footsteps move towards the door. I heard him yell at the guard in Farsi, telling him to come and get this dog – me – and throw him back in his cage – my solitary cell. Panic fell over me. I don't want to go back to that grave. While I feel like I'm good at calling bluffs, his threats are becoming more realistic to me now. What if he really does leave me here? Oh God, please don't put me back in there! I am angry and growing desperate.

"Haji, what the hell are you talking about! You can't keep me here! I didn't do anything! I don't know what you want from me!" I yell, hoping he hears it.

He doesn't. He's gone. Two guards rushed in, each one grabbing an elbow. I got up and pulled my arms away.

"Get your hands off of me!"

"Shut your mouth and get back in your cell!" he yelled at me.

They both pulled on my elbows and pushed me at a sprinted pace, shoving me in the back with the batons as they barreled me back towards my cell. Halfway there, while handcuffed and blindfolded, I fell from the baton push in the back, and trip over the cheap, plastic sandals on my feet. My shoulder hits the cold concrete floor. They scream at me to get up and grab me by my elbows again to pull me up. I can see my cell door, and I begin to panic. I don't want to go back in there. You die every minute in there. I tried to plant my feet to prevent them from putting me in my cell, but without my hands, I'm unsuccessful. One guard holds me as the other opens my cell and together shove me on the back, and the cell door slams shut behind me.

I focused on one part of the door and stared at it for several minutes. I can't move. I literally can't move, and I fixate on the door. After several minutes, I break down and cry. It's not a cry. It's more of a wail. It's slow, deep, and without tears. It's as if somewhere deep inside had been torn open, and all of the pain was pouring out. I slowly crumble. First, my chin was going into my chest. Then my legs weaken, and I fall to my knees in front of the door. I intertwine my fingers like I'm praying and push my hands against the door. I finally rest my forehead on my hands. I realize that I am all alone.

The next morning, I'm woken up for my breakfast of stale bread, margarine, and tea by a young guard. This 24-year-old guard was easy going with me and would ask me how I was doing and smile. I could tell he wasn't a bad person; he was probably the son of someone in the Basij forces whose dad got him a job at the MOI detention center. His father was one of those fathers that wanted his son to follow in his footsteps, not caring whether his son wants to or not. This guard spoke a few words of English to me and seemed like someone that secretly watched the black market American movies and listened to banned music but would deny it if they found out.

Under the guise of dropping off food or doing routine checks, after checking that no one else was around, he would open the latch at the top of my door and ask me questions. How does one buy a house in America? What's the process for buying a car? How old were people when they moved out of their parents' homes there? I could tell he still lived at home like most young Iranians. Sometimes I grew irritated with these questions. I was in the pits of hell, unable to talk to my family, or even get fresh air, and he was asking me about the process of buying a car in America! After weeks of solitary confinement, I began looking forward to his questions. I just wanted to see another person, exchange a few words, and feel like I was still alive.

The young guard always spoke with great caution and incredible fear as he knew the consequences would be grave if his superiors suspected him of being a sympathizer. At one point, he even asked me if I would act as a reference for him to get a visa when I returned to the United States, so he too could leave Iran. I thought to myself that I'd be happy to bring him to the United States and direct him to the finest maximum security prison America has to offer. At other times, I thought that maybe under different circumstances, this guy would be no different than any young American I'd run into back home. I doubted that he shared many of the ideals that were force-fed to him as a young person.

He had never left the country, grew up in a small rural area of Tehran, and this was all he knew. He didn't understand that there was a life out there different than the lifestyle forced on him. However, movies, TV, social networks, and the internet seemed to have an impact on him. The idea of being able to walk around a city like New York City and be able to express yourself any way you wanted amazed him. To choose what, when, and how he wanted to live his life, and see immigrants from all different countries coming to the United States and succeeding was something that boggled his mind.

The guard thought about the little bread and jam that he ate for breakfast, the rice bowl that he would have for lunch, and a little soup that he would scarf down for dinner, and began to get depressed over what he knew would be his future in Iran. He drove a Chinese motorcycle to and from the prison, sometimes sharing with another soldier who drove with him. He would ask me about magazine pictures of different cars; Ford Mustangs were his favorite. I told him this car was OK, and ownership was easy with a car loan and a few grand. He was shocked. He was probably riding a small chinese motorcycle common in Iran, and sleeping on the floor in his parents' living room.

His social life was to go to the almost daily religious events with his father or other basijis. I could tell that he was very depressed at the prospects of his future and the monotony that would follow him until he was an older man. While his father had fought in the Iran-Iraq war and was deeply involved in the Islamic revolution, he wasn't. He had heard stories his whole life and told to cry over the deaths of those who went before him that he never knew – the martyrs, a popular topic among the religious in Iran. Despite having been indoctrinated from a young age, I could tell his heart wasn't involved in all of it. He was bound by the social pressures around him to think, dress, and do the things that his father told him to do.

Deep down inside, though, he was curious. He wanted to see what life was like outside of his bubble. I could almost see his imagination dreaming of walking in New York City, or on a beach in Los Angeles. He would have a car – a Ford Mustang convertible and would be cruising the streets, maybe an American girl – blond-haired and blue-eyed – in the passenger seat. His name was probably Hasan, but he'd go by "Hank" and listen to 2pac instead of the religious chants that had been bludgeoning his ears since he was a young boy. My talks with the young guard made me realize how twisted this regime was and how terribly it treated its people. On the one hand, I had this young man who, despite dressing and acting like a Basiji hardliner, was a closet American. On the other hand, I had Haji, who thought that he was carrying out God's will by torturing people and making up both law and religion as he went along.

Chapter Nine:
The Barking of the Dog

One morning, I waited for my pills to arrive after breakfast as usual, but was surprised that they never did. I waited for an hour before pushing a button in my cell that would turn on a light outside my door, indicating to the guards I needed something. Thirty minutes later, the guard finally came to the door. When I asked for my pills, he shut the hatch without giving me an answer. I began to feel uneasy. As much as I pretended that I didn't need them, they had become a powerful coping mechanism for me. I thought this need made me weak, but these were extraordinary circumstances. I desperately needed sleep, and this was the only way it found me.

I paced around my small cell. I knocked on the wall to engage with the prisoner in the next cell over. I relived memories. I was trying to do everything I could to distract my mind from my need for my pills. I knew something wasn't right. I felt like there was a fire burning inside of me. This place worked like clockwork unless it was the inmate making the request, then it was when they felt like being bothered. Where were my pills? They always came after breakfast. Why were they not here?

Time passed. The worries that the pills silenced began to scream at me. The walls of the cell began to close in on me slowly. The fire building inside of me went from candle, to raging inferno. Not having my pills was no longer the problem, at least the only problem.

Everything was cause for concern. Every second felt like an hour. Little ticks began as I kept running my hands through my hair, stretching against the wall, splashing water on my face, pacing the room, slamming the side of my hands against the wall, and angrily knocking the wall to alert the prisoner next to me. An hour later, I hit the light again.

"Where is my medicine? It was supposed to be here a few hours ago!"

The guard gave me an annoyed look and closed the hatch again without giving me an answer. The dismissal infuriated me. As soon as he closed the hatch, I pounded the door in revolt. I'm facing a dilemma. My gut was telling me to rattle the door, make some noise, and demand that the doctor or nurse see me and give me my pills. I hadn't forgotten the blows of the batons, the shocks of the taser at my kidneys, or the pain my hands felt after being handcuffed to the pipe in my cell for hours.

I toughed it out for a few hours more, but I was really on fire now. What I was feeling was more than a mental setback solved with mental fortitude. This was a physiological response. I felt like I was being burned alive, and the pills were the only thing that could put this fire out. This pain was excruciating. It was stronger than the threat of retribution I faced from the guards, so I began to slam and kick the door and yell for a guard. A few other prisoners had joined me. A few minutes later, the hatch on the door opens.

"I want to see the doctor! Where are my freaking pills! I'll keep banging this door until I get some answers!", I yelled.

"Do you want us to come back in there and chain you to the wall!" he barked back.

I can tell that my comment angered him, but he shut the hatch, and nothing happened. I could hear him arguing with someone at the end of the hall and expected him to come back with more guards any minute. I figured I would take a beating, but at this point, I didn't care; I was exploding on the inside. The cell reminded me of a fiction novel I read once where a man was kidnapped and put in a decompression chamber. His torturer would slowly increase the pressure and then suddenly drop it while he videotaped the effect this had on his victims'. I felt like I was going to implode like the victims in the novel. I would have welcomed death.

If I died, if I used my clothes and figured out some way to hang myself or a way to slit my wrist, it would all end. I couldn't bring myself to entertain the idea for more than a few minutes though. Each time I went down that dark road in my mind, I thought of my family. I saw my mother and father's faces after hearing the news that I'd committed suicide in prison. Would they even send my body home? I thought of my reputation as a Marine. I imagined the headline, "Former US Marine commits suicide in an Iranian prison." Most people would probably think I died by nefarious means. What if I did make it out of here? What if I could return home with my head held high and had the chance to tell the world that they didn't defeat me? My sounder judgment was kicking in. "Get those thoughts out of your head, Amir! I'm coming out of this! I'm going home; I'm going home." This became my mantra.

I said a prayer that I read in the Quran: "God does not burden a soul except with that which is within its capacity." A particular verse struck a chord with me, "Oh Lord, do not impose on us if we have forgotten or have erred. Oh Lord, do not lay upon us a burden like that which you laid upon those before us. Oh Lord, and do not burden us with which we have no ability to bear." My imprisonment in Iran would test the meaning of this verse to the fullest.

I needed God's help. There was no way I could handle this on my own. The guards ignored me for two days. Despite laying down on my back in front of the door and kicking it for hours, no one came. No one. I kicked and yelled for hours. Even the other prisoners who had originally made noise in solidarity with me had gone silent. When a guard finally opened the hatch to give me the evening meal, I pleaded to see the doctor. He slammed the door shut again. I couldn't understand why they wouldn't just give me the damn pills. I was so dehydrated from my yelling; I chugged as much water from the sink as I could. Eventually, I passed out from exhaustion.

I later discovered that the drug given to me in Ward 209 was a high dose of lithium, along with 3 other tiny pills that to this day I have no idea what they were. Lithium is a very powerful antidepressant that requires constant monitoring from a psychiatrist that includes blood tests done regularly to check toxicity levels. I had no monitoring, and I didn't have a psychiatrist.

Instead, my captors used it as a way to torture me and gain my cooperation. They created an addiction to force me to go through withdrawal. Withdrawal symptoms from Lithium include irritability, mania, anxiety, suicidal ideation, depressions, and flu-like symptoms. Experiencing withdrawal symptoms along with the physical and psychological impact of solitary confinement after months of isolation, torture, and beatings in a foreign country with no one to help me only exacerbated my feelings of desperation and fear.

For several days, I pleaded with the guards, but no pills arrived. I was left to feel the many psychological and physical symptoms inside my thick cell walls alone. One day my cell door was opened, and several guards yelled at me to come out blindfolded. I had a feeling I knew where I was going. I had hoped I was going to see the doctor, but I quickly realized I was going to the interrogation room. I had a visitor.

I was told to stand outside the interrogation room facing the wall and stay roughly six inches from the wall. Despite my protests, I was forced to stand here for several hours. The guards came and told me to sit down. At this point, nearly four months had gone by in solitary confinement. I endured beatings, sensory deprivation, had dirty water thrown into my cell when I would sleep, and was currently going through chemical induced withdrawals. I was beginning to believe the threats that Haji made every time he visited me and that I would be trapped in Evin Prison until my hair became as white as my teeth. I had no way of knowing how much longer this was going to continue. I felt like my health was deteriorating rapidly, not only my physical but mental health. I was concerned about committing suicide. I felt like something fundamental was changing about me from the isolation and treatment I endured.

As they took me into the interrogation room, I told myself that I was going to try to come to some agreement with Haji. I had my pride, but what good would it do me if my health was compromised or if I never left this place? I had to do something because my current path was only getting me solitary and beatings. Plus, I badly wanted my medication. I desperately needed to sleep to let my mind shut off, but I knew that without the pills, that would never happen.

Without the pills, I would continue to suffer. As tough as someone can be, there is always a point where being practical has to come before being prideful, where the loss outweighs the gain, where we accept a tactical surrender in hopes that we can regroup and try to fight back another time. Now was the time. The footsteps came closer and Haji walked in.

"Amir agha, how are you? Good?" he breezily asked.

This angered me. I knew he was trying to get a rise out of me. "Alhamdulillah - praise be to God," I responded.

I wanted to remain calm even though I knew he was getting detailed reports on my every move. I knew he was also receiving visual and audio surveillance of me. The cells had tiny cameras that were barely visible to the naked eye.

"Amir, we're growing tired of you. You've wasted our time. If you think this is as bad as it gets in here, you're wrong. We can make life much, much worse for you. I'm only going to give you one last chance to cooperate. This is it, Amir. Up until now, have I done everything I said I would do?"

I didn't respond.

"I always make good on my promises. Whatever it is, I say I'm going to do, I do. So what's it going to be?"

I think for a minute and decide I'm going to try and get him to reveal what exactly it was that he wanted.

"Maybe I want to cooperate with you, but I don't know how to cooperate with you. I've been in solitary for a long time now. Please help me understand this."

"Amir, you're hurting yourself. We know everything. We don't need you to tell us, but if you want to help yourself, you should. You work for the CIA, Amir. That's why you are here, and you will stay here until you talk." Haji told me.

"And if I tell you I work for the CIA, what happens?" I asked. I just needed to get home. I could correct this narrative once I was outside of Iran. Haji tells me that if I cooperate, I'll be able to call my family and will be on the first plane back home.

"Promise you'll let me make a phone call and tell them to give me my pills."

I heard creaks from movement in the chairs they were sitting in once I said this, as they most likely were happy that they had "cracked" me. Haji's tone changed. He went from threatening to friendly rather quickly.

"I promise," he said. "You'll get to call anyone you like. Tell your family you're ok, and we will release you. You'll be on a plane back to the USA in no time."

"You're right Haji, I work for the CIA, they sent me here like you said, I want to cooperate."

I hear Haji stand up and walk slowly over to me. "Just write it down here so I know you are serious about cooperating, and so I can process your release. Write one line that you are CIA, and sign."

Doubts and anxiety are racing through my mind about writing this line,, but before I let those thoughts flood my brain, and talk me out of it I grab the pen and quickly write the sentence that would set me free, or so I thought.

Haji walked over and patted me on the shoulder and said that I made the right decision. He puts a cup of tea and some sugar cubes in front of me. "Drink your tea and relax. I'm going to come and see you again soon. I'll tell the doctor to give you your pills."

Haji leaves the room. The guards come and take me to my cell, and the nurse appears and hands me my pills. I rip them from his hands and swallow them down immediately. Like the helicopter that pours water on a fire from above, the flames inside had been extinguished. With each second the drugs enter my blood and travel through my body, I feel more and more relaxed. Those invisible hands again rise from the cell floor and drag me down to the corner where I can gaze at the wall and try to escape this place to a nice memory or a better place. I try to relax with the hopes that I'll fall asleep. My eyelids get heavier, and in no time, all is dark.

Chapter Ten

Pasdaran Avenue

The next morning a guard opens the door an hour after breakfast and tells me to wrap up my blankets and bring them with me. Anything indicating me leaving this cell doesn't require me asking any questions. I'm just happy to leave. With my blindfold back on, I follow him to the end of the hall, where I drop my blankets. I'm taken outside of the facility and led down steps to a waiting vehicle. The vehicle takes me back to the place where I was processed. I'm given back my clothes and told to put them on. I'm getting optimistic now, happy to be out of that horror house, happy to be dressed in my own clothes, and happy to be taking off the pathetic prison pajamas that made me just another piece of prison property.

The MOI guards escorted me into a van with curtains covering the windows. I'm without my blindfold. This is a good sign. As we drive out the gate, I look at the opening in the window and see all of the mothers, fathers, brothers, and sisters waiting behind a wall trying to find out what has happened to their loved ones. I could only imagine what my family was going through at the time. My family in Iran, worried about me, and my family in America, terrified. We zipped through Tehran's traffic for fifteen minutes until we arrived at a residential area. They order me to put my blindfold back on.

These guards were the Ministry of Intelligence agents, different from the guards who ran the prison, fed me three times a day, and doled out my punishments. Each time I left the prison grounds, I was on loan from the prison to the MOI. They would become responsible for me. A few minutes later, the sliding door opened, and I'm led out. All I can see are my feet. Up a few steps, and we walk into what appears to be a residence.

Once inside, I'm allowed to take my blindfold off. I can see the residence I'm in is a nice one as I walk over clean, shiny travertine tile. I turn right into what appears to be a living room with a table and a bowl of fresh fruit waiting for me. There's a pen, paper, and on the wall hangs a large photo of Ayatollah Khamenei, the Supreme Leader of Iran. They put me into a chair facing a wall, and a few minutes later, I hear Haji behind me say hello.

"Amir agha, I told you I do whatever I say. I told you I'd help you if you cooperated." "Did I help you?"

"You're not in prison anymore right? Please have some fruit." I hesitantly grab a pear and slice it with my plastic knife.

Haji continues, "What we want is for you to do is help us with a training video. Think of it as role-playing. An interviewer will ask you some questions, and you will know how to answer.

Tell them the CIA recruited you for a mission to infiltrate sensitive areas in Iran, get information, and implicate us in terrorist activities. You didn't do it. We stopped you, so don't worry. You didn't commit any crime. The CIA sent you here. All this was a horrible mistake they made. You'll make the video to help us with training; it will never be seen in public. You do this, you go home, and if you don't, you go back to solitary, and I promise Amir, I will never come back and give you another chance. You'll stay there until your hair becomes as white as your teeth. We wrote some questions on forms for you to answer to prepare you for the interview. Answer them in writing, we will give you a day or two."

I feel ridiculous sitting there eating fruit while Haji fed me his lies, but I hadn't had any fruit or fresh food for several months. I hadn't noticed just how hungry I was in prison with all the stress, and anxiety, but for the first time my appetite had returned. I was trying not to show my eagerness to devour what was in front of me. Haji told me that he would take me to see my relatives in Iran and then straight to the airport so I can return home. Hearing him say those words felt like jumping into a cold pool on a hot summer day. Those words were a relief. Liberation. A light at the end of this dark road. It meant that this nightmare would be over. It didn't matter that in my gut, I was worried I was being lied to by Haji. The important thing was that I wasn't in solitary, I was eating fruit, and for once, Haji was talking to me about freedom and airports, instead of pain and suffering.

Haji left, and the guards took me down into the basement of the residence. Behind a fortified metal door was a large room with a bed, television, and shower. There were bars on the windows and no other way out of the room. In the corner were tiny cameras. The door shut behind me, and I found myself locked up again. I realized that this was a safe house or secret prison. The Ministry of Intelligence had safe houses like this all over the city; many left over from the SAVAK - Iran's intelligence service under the Shah. In the room, next to the bed was a small desk with a notepad and pen. I had 24 hours to write about what happened and why I was in Iran.

Every few hours, a guard would drop off a thermos with tea, fruit, and takeout Persian food. One meal had an address on it from a takeout restaurant on Pasdaran Avenue, a major street that cuts through Tehran. I would later come to learn when I explained what happened to fellow inmates that this street also happens to house the headquarters of Iran's Ministry of Intelligence. The guards didn't pay much attention to detail because they went to great lengths to conceal where I was. The food was still quite hot, so I knew it was picked up by a location nearby. The exact address of the restaurant on the package gave me an idea of where I was. Later, in conversation with one of the guards, he asked me if I thought their work was professional compared to Americans. I told him I didn't know because they transported prisoners, and I didn't have any experience with that. I told him that seeing that they didn't want me to know where I was, they probably shouldn't have given me food with the address of the restaurant on a container. His face drained from embarrassment, and he quickly shut the door. I probably shouldn't have told him that I roughly knew where I was, but I couldn't resist the opportunity to make this MOI agent feel incompetent.

The television inside the room was not connected to an antenna or satellite. It only played DVDs from an attached DVD player. The ironic part of this was that the movies available to me were all blockbuster movies from America. Rocky, Rambo, Terminator II, and Vicky Cristina Barcelona. Iran often accuses America of infiltrating Iran and trying to create a soft revolution through music, movies, and academic work. They will use the possession of these materials as a reason for an arrest. Here I was, a "guest" of the Ministry of Intelligence, and they were giving me the same works they use to condemn ordinary Iranians. I had had enough of action and violence the past several months in Evin Prison, so I chose to watch Vicky Cristina Barcelona. Scenes with Scarlette Johanson and Penelope Cruz brought me calm, and I began to feel more hopeful about my return home. I watched the movie while I wrote the responses to the papers Haji gave. Now that my situation had improved and I was no longer in a state of constant panic as I was in solitary, my logic began to return. What if this was all just an elaborate scheme to extract a false confession? What if I was hanging myself by writing these words? If this was just for a training video, why did I need to sign with signature, and thumb print? These questions were always bouncing in my mind, but I had lost all fear of negative consequences at this point. I blocked the reasoning from my mind, and just went along. I wrote that I was a CIA agent, sent by the CIA to infiltrate the government of Iran in terrorist activities. I did, however, decide to write a disclaimer sentence at the end of each document. The disclaimer read, "I, Amir Hekmati am writing these things because I am told by Haji that if I do I will be released, not because they are true, they are not."

Twenty-four hours later, a guard says Haji wanted to speak with me upstairs. With my blindfold on, I went upstairs and sat in my chair again, facing the picture of Iran's supreme leader.

Haji had reviewed my papers and said, "This is how you want to write?" "This is no good. This is garbage. Write it again." He shuffled the papers some more. "I'll give you one more shot. But, Amir, you must know that my patience is running thin. We brought you here, showed you hospitality, and this is how you repay us? Start over and do it right this time, otherwise, I'm taking you back to Evin prison, and I will never see you again."

Haji didn't give me a chance to respond. He stormed out of the room. I didn't understand what he was doing or why until I was moved to a different ward in Evin Prison. I was shocked that this was really the government of Iran engaging in blatant coercion of a detainee. I could've imagined this in a cheap movie, but was this really happening? A government agent can just beat you into writing whatever he says? Many months later I would learn just how bad things were in Iran in a joke told to me by an Iranian inmate. As an attempt to cheer me up, an older prisoner told me a joke about the American, Israel, and Iranian intelligence agencies:

He said, "The Americans, the Israelis, and the Iranians have a competition to see who can catch the rabbit first. The Americans catch the rabbit in 10 minutes, the Israelis catch the rabbit in 15 minutes, and the Iranians catch the rabbit in 2 minutes. Everyone is stunned as to how the Iranians were able to beat the US and Israelis by so much and find the rabbit so fast. They ask the Iranians to show them the rabbit, and the Iranians open the trunk of the vehicle, and they all look at a huge Bear! The Americans and Israelis chuckle and say, "This is a bear, not a rabbit!"

The Iranian responds confidently by saying, "No, ask him yourself." The Israelis and the Americans say, "What are you?!

The bear with a bloody nose and smashed teeth responds, "I'm a rabbit! My mother is a rabbit; my father is a rabbit!"

We see the extent of the MOI's intelligence prowess summed up in threat, torture, lawlessness, and brute force. Yes the rumors were true. If they wanted to they could do anything they wanted, literally. They would just as easily find some religious, or political justification to do so. I learned that it wasn't that the agents, and their organization had no conscience, it was that they actually believed to be righteous in their actions. In some twisted way, they were actually 'allowed' to do these things, and were serving god by doing so. Beginning to understand my captors made me feel like a prisoner not only inside the walls of Evin, but inside the twisted ideology of their radical minds. I was convinced there were few worse places on earth than this prison within a prison of sorts. God help me.

⌧

Chapter Eleven:
Scripted and Coerced Confessions

"I'll give you another 48 hours, and then you go back to solitary. Now go back down and write it all over again from the beginning. You've left everything out. The last part you must write to help us and help yourself. Write your mission, mission for the CIA," Haji told me when he made another appearance at the safe house.

"What mission? You keep talking about my mission. I just want to go home and see my family. I've explained this to you for months now. I'm 27! Until I came to visit my family, I had never stepped foot in Iran in my life! The three weeks that I was here before you arrested me, I was with my family, and you know it! Have you been watching those James Bond movies and thought they are real? Do you think I can fly into Iran and do whatever I want? What is my supposed mission? What do you mean spying? Spying on what? Do I have pictures of something I shouldn't? Documents? Do you think it's that easy? That I just fly in and you catch someone working for the CIA? This is a freakin' joke." I'm frustrated. I'm angry. I just want to go home and see my family."

"No, Amir, this is no joke," Haji says. "This isn't America. This isn't Switzerland. This is the Islamic Republic of Iran. I, do you hear me, I, say who is and who isn't a spy in this country. No lawyer, no judge, no trial. Just me. I decide about your life. Do you doubt me? Don't you understand? For the last four months, no one could do anything for you. I say that you are a spy, then you are a spy. You only say yes to me. That's it. You're a spy for the CIA. Your mission was to infiltrate Iran's intelligence service, create a network of spies, and find a way to accuse Iran's government of being involved in terrorist activities. You received training before you came to Iran to undertake this mission. Now go write! I'll be back in 48 hours. If all goes well, you'll be flying home on an airplane. Mess this up, and you will rot in that cell." He pats me on the shoulder and then walks out.

The guard takes me downstairs where a fresh notebook and new pen sit on the desk to see if I write things differently this second time around without the original statement as a reference. He keeps talking about 48 hours. Maybe arrangements for my departure had already been made. So, I sit down, drink tea, and write again. I write and write. I'm emotionally, mentally, and physically exhausted. I've lost 25 pounds that I didn't have to lose. I miss my family. I want this nightmare to be over. He's right, though, this isn't America. This place isn't even as good as some abandoned landfill in the USA, and he can forget about Switzerland. I didn't have any rights here, and life here isn't valued by the Ministry of Intelligence anyway. The people in the detention center were Iranians from Iran. Why would he care about an American of Iranian descent?

I decided to write whatever he said and be done with it. Whatever happened as a result of this couldn't be worse than the hell I had been living in already. I knew my limit and knew that I couldn't handle much more of this. If I didn't write now, I might face another month of torture to get answers out of me. The difference is that now I've lost more weight and my health wouldn't be the only thing that could get damaged. I wrote, drank tea, ate Iranian take-out that the guards brought me, prayed for my life and freedom, and watched a DVD. After the 48 hours had passed, like clockwork, I was summoned again. As soon as I sat down, I could hear Haji scanning my documents. He had told me if I had not given him the answers he needed, I would find myself back in solitary. As he read, my anxiety grew. I couldn't go back to that place. Not again. After five minutes, Haji finally speaks.

"Ok, Amir, you did ok, not great, but I'll spare you solitary for now. I can't send you home looking like this. We're going to take you to a nice hotel where you can shave and shower.

We'll have some clothes there for you, and whatever else you need. We'll go to the hotel, and we'll take what you've written and go through it one more time. We want you to help us with a training video, just have a dialogue with one of our guys about what you wrote. This is for our internal training purposes. We need this to close the file and to be done with you."

My heart sinks as I ponder the prospect of going on camera. What if this is misused? Put on air? "I'm sorry I can't do anything on camera. We've seen all the stuff you've put out before in the news back home. Anytime someone goes on camera, they are paraded on television and given a harsh sentence."

"Like who?" Haji asks.

"The 3 American Hikers, the Embassy hostages, this guy, Rigi."

"You're not Rigi," he responds.

Abdul Malik Rigi was a Baluch separatist who carried out several bombings inside Iran and assassinated several of Iran's Revolutionary Guard commanders.

He was right. I'm not Rigi. I'm just visiting. I've not killed anyone. I've done nothing.

"Amir agha, you're almost finished. Don't mess this up. Cooperate, and let's get this down and send you home. We don't like to be here either."

I stay silent, and he accepts my silence as agreement.

To not raise suspicions, for the first time since my initial arrest, I'm allowed to move without handcuffs, blindfold, and in my own clothes. The guards escort me to the same van outside with covered windows. Before we stepped out, the agent showed me his 9mm pistol and told me he didn't want to have to use it. He told me to be calm, not to yell or pass on information to anyone, and that if I run, he will shoot me. I looked at him without saying anything and just sort of nodded. The simple freedom of walking in an open area without handcuffs is the most exhilarating feeling I had felt in months. A breeze crawling over the mountaintops cooled by the snow caps gave me my first breath of fresh air in five months. Everything about Evin is different. It's like a sauna with open sewage. I appreciate this simple but amazing blessing from nature. I get into the van, and we depart.

A short ride later, I see on my right a luxury hotel and on my left the mountain ranges surrounding Tehran. We arrive at Hotel Esteghlal. One guard walked 15 steps ahead of me, one beside me, and two walking 15 steps behind. They are all wearing overcoats to conceal their firearms. Once we are inside, I see guests lounging in the lobby. The lobby smelled of fresh pastries and tea. I wondered if the international guests staying there knew that Iran's Ministry of Intelligence likes taking care of business there and what they would think if they found out?

Would they care about what I had been through the past five months?

I looked at them as though they were from another world, the "free" world, and I was just a visitor. I envied their carelessness, sitting free while playing with their smartphones, sipping coffee, eating a meal of their choice, and talking to one another. I wanted to start yelling that my name is Amir Hekmati, I'm being held captive by the Ministry of Intelligence, and I want to go home. I figured that if I did, the agents would rush me, and I would have to answer to Haji for the next six months or so, or worse, they would make me disappear. The agents are apprehensive, though, as if they can read my mind. They surrounded me now, one agent continuously talking to me to gauge my emotional state and look for any clues as to what I might do.

We finally approached the elevator, and the five of us packed inside. I think that most people in prison or other dangerous environments adapt, and hyper-vigilance becomes second nature. I could see that the guards were visibly nervous. I looked to see what floor we were going to. Were they taking me to the top floor because it would be harder for me to escape? Does the Ministry of Intelligence have an agreement with the hotel, and the top floor belongs to them? Were they planning on throwing me off the roof once this was all done?

We entered a luxurious hotel room with a big living area and a separate bedroom with a large study. Once inside, I am sent to the bathroom to shave and shower. Once I finish, I sit in the living room with the agents and a man that introduced himself as an interviewer for the training video. I would later see him on television as a reporter for Iran's State television network.

On the table in front of me is a bowl of fruit, some beverages, and a pack of cigarettes. While I wasn't a smoker, after the stress I'd endured over the past five months, I graciously accepted the smokes. I was happy to have anything that would bring me any kind of relief. I deeply inhaled, desperate to feel the nicotine hit me. The guards and reporter looked at me in amazement as I inhaled the smoke to the depths of my lungs, and held it. I skipped the fruit and downed the beverage – a non-alcoholic beer – while I lit another cigarette.

A few minutes later, the agent speaks to someone in the doorway. After their conversation, he tells me to get up, and we go to a side room where he moves a chair to face the wall. I'm a professional at this by now. I knew who would be coming into the room. Just once I wanted to catch a glimpse of his face and to look eye-to-eye with the man responsible for stealing five years of my life. Did he look like a villain in a movie, or did he look like an uncle you would sit across and play chess with at a family gathering? I will never know.

"Amir agha, you're almost there. If this training video goes well, you'll be on your way to the airport. I can't give you lots of details, but your family is very worried about you. Make this easy on you and them. I don't want to see you like this. Believe me. It hurts me, too; you're a young man with a bright future."

I know he's feeding me lies. I'm in a position where I want to believe what he says –where I need to believe what he says. The alternative was returning to solitary, and that was not an option for me if I could help it. I inhaled one more cigarette before we begin. The reporter asked his questions, and I repeated the script that I had written at the safehouse and that Haji had approved. The interview is over twenty minutes later, and I feel optimistic. I imagine myself sitting on the plane and looking down at this place with a sigh of relief that I was going home.

"I've given you your stupid video and did everything you said. Where is Haji? When do I get the hell out of here?" I asked one of the agents.

"Haji had to leave to take care of some things and prepare for your departure. We are going back to the safe house. Once we get everything wrapped up, we can take you to the airport."

"What? That wasn't the deal! Haji said we'd leave from this hotel. I don't want to go and sit in the basement of that house again." I was angry.

"Calm down! He is preparing for your departure. It's not that easy. I will have Haji come to the house and speak with you. We need to leave now. Come on, let's go."

A new day rises, and then it falls. It repeats. Each day, I argue with the agent and look for any clue as to why I had not left yet. There had been no visits with Haji. With no Haji in sight, I started doubting my return home. I did everything I could to convince myself that soon I would be out of Iran and home in Michigan. Finally, on the sixth day in the basement of the safehouse, the agent opens the door and tells me to gather my things because we are leaving. I'm thrilled! I hurry to pack up and am ready to leave finally. I get in the van that will take me to the airport. Soon this nightmare will be over! I could imagine my families' smiling faces. I smile back.

As we drive through Tehran's streets, I cannot see to the left of me or the right of me because of the curtains in the van. I can see in front of me, though, and continue to look for clues that we are heading towards the airport - a billboard, a sign. After driving for twenty minutes, I feel a terrible pain in my stomach as I see a familiar path in front of me. It is the path that I traveled after being arrested at my uncle's home. I realized that we were not heading to the airport. My suspicions were confirmed when I saw the rusty sign of Evin Prison on the highway overpass. I read it as "Welcome to hell."

Chapter Twelve

Evin, Again

Any happy thoughts I imagined of reuniting with my family were replaced with thoughts of that grave of a cell and the misery that took place inside of it. The only comfort I had was that I was convinced there was nothing else I could have done. Like Déjà vu, I said the same prayer that I did when I first entered Evin. I asked God for strength that I didn't have yet. Once again, the in-processing took place. This time I didn't put up a fight. I said nothing to the guards. My only communication to them was a look of contempt - a look that was worse than a thousand insults. I needed to conserve my energy, and this time as I entered the prison and moved towards my cell, I felt something change inside of me. My DNA was adjusting so that I could adapt and endure.

Part of me realized that the best way to defeat these walls was to become like them. No emotion, no worry, no panic. Solid. Solid like the walls that enclosed me. I pretended that I was born in Evin. I had no family, no previous life, no history. I was of this cell, I live in this cell, and I die in this cell. Nothing else existed. I no longer kicked the door in protest. I no longer asked for Haji; he was dead to me. The guards would give me strange looks, desperately wanting to see me upset. I took satisfaction in not letting them see that I was upset.

I knew that to survive, I had to eat, even if it was the garbage that they fed us. I began eating all my food and asking for seconds.

Ordinarily, there were no seconds in Evin Prison. They had the exact number of meals for the exact number of prisoners that day. Now and again, though, another prisoner would go on hunger strike. If the guard was in a good mood, he would give me that prisoner's portion. I would ask at each meal if there was any more. I would ask the same when it came to bread. The stale sheet bread that they gave us helped fill me up at night, and ease the severe hunger I endured prior to going to bed each night. I worried about the long-term use of the pills and if it would harm my stomach lining, particularly if I took them on an empty stomach. If I could have extra bread, maybe it would act as a buffer.

After breakfast, I would workout. Squats, stretches, pushups, jumping in place - anything to get my heart rate up and my blood circulating. Every night my body filled with the poison of that place, and every morning I tried to purge it with exercise. Once I was all sweaty and felt better, I'd take a shower using my hand and the sink water. I'd take off my prison-issued shirt, splash water on myself, use the tiny soap bar, and clean up. This ritual helped me deal with the quiet tediousness of the rest of the day. After my sink shower, I would read the Quran, or Keys to Heaven book placed in each cell, and the only allowed reading material. That didn't stop me from asking them for new books every few days. Asking for books everyday was one form of rebellion I took pride in. The guards would always get annoyed by the question, and look at me strangely, wondering if the only concern I had in continued solitary was inadequate reading material.

Sometimes I would read the text of the religious scripts; other times, I would try to memorize the verses, not paying attention to the content. I would count the verses or letters on any given page and then play little math games in my head. I was trying to keep my brain alive because I felt like it was dying from not being used. I have always been an active person. Staring at these walls was difficult. This kind of brain play helped me get through the day. I tried to break the day up into tiny pieces, so the road ahead of me wouldn't look so long. At breakfast, I focused on getting to lunch. At lunch, I focused on getting to dinner. At dinner, I focused on finding a way to fall asleep.

Each time I would lay down to sleep, I tried my best to think positive. This was one more day towards the end of this road. The end was still unknown, but it was one day less, anyway. I tried to console myself as I fell asleep. At night is when the horrors of my experience at Evin would visit me. In the end, I made my prayers, prayed for my family, and managed to fall asleep. I would wake up each morning, ready to do my ritual all over again. "After each dark night is a bright morning."

Many months later, at times Ward 209 would reach capacity, and they were forced to add a prisoner or two to my already tiny cell for a day or two. They always did so reluctantly, and kept checking in. Often they'd pull the prisoner out, and ask what I told him. I was counseled to not tell anyone who I was, but I always did in hopes word would get out to my family. One day the door swung open, and in came another detainee.

He was a 24-year-old young man and a professional thief. To protect his identity, I'll refer to him as Reza. Reza's modus operandi was to ride on the back of a motorcycle with his accomplice and scout vehicles that had open windows or unlocked doors where a purse, briefcase, or anything of value could be quickly grabbed from the vehicle as they sped away. Considering Tehran's heavy traffic, someone on a motorcycle can make a getaway much easier than someone in a vehicle. The motorcycle helmet gave perfect cover without raising suspicion, and the tag on the motorcycle was easily counterfeited. This unlucky thief, however, stole a briefcase containing a laptop, smartphone, and classified documents belonging to an Iranian Intelligence agent.

Reza was only interested in making a quick profit. He sold the laptop, and smartphone to a local vendor for $70, and claims to have ditched the documents. After months of serious investigation on behalf of Iranian intelligence, they were able to track the laptop and smartphone to the local vendor who identified the thief.

The thief, Reza, was sitting in the cell with me and described coming outside one day to get on his motorcycle. He lived with his girlfriend in a tiny apartment in Shush, a lower-income area of Tehran. Reza told me how much he loved his girlfriend and missed taking her for rides on the back of his motorcycle while they were high on crystal meth.

Crystal meth was quickly becoming the drug of choice for young Iranians. It gave them an intense high, increased sex drive, and was very effective at helping them escape the depression that has gripped young people in Tehran. They were not only suffering from an impossible job and economic situation, but from a lack of socialization. Looking at Tehran through a young person's eyes, you saw war, death chants, and morality police nearby to ask you who the woman you are walking with is or tell you to go home and change your clothes. Any objection could quickly turn ugly. Many have been beaten or put on blacklists barring them from public services.

Reza had just enjoyed a night of partying at an apartment in Tehran, where everyone was high on crystal meth. He left the apartment early in the morning to start his day job as a parcel deliverer. In Tehran, the youth can find daily work in taking letters, items, and giving rides to people on the back of their motorcycle. As he left the apartment, he noticed a Samand with tinted windows at the end of the alleyway. He noticed it because it was out of place. As he approached his motorcycle, the car accelerated into the alleyway with several plainclothes officers and a mullah running behind it. Behind him was a dead-end, so he tried to run past them like a wide-receiver but was clotheslined by a big officer in a suit. He said the mullah took off his sandals, and began hitting him in the head with it while he was roughed up and thrown in the back of the car by the plainclothes officers.

Afterward, Reza was taken to the same part of Evin I was, and put in solitary confinement. After being thoroughly beaten and tortured for 41 days, including having several of his rear teeth knocked out, he entered my cell and began to tell his story. As a meth addict, he was losing it in prison. At this point, I had been in Evin prison for many months, almost all in solitary confinement. When he asked how long I had been there and I told him, he kept saying "Khaylee mardee" - You're a real man. Reza told me he'd been arrested many times before and did time for stealing. He said these were just city cops, and not intelligence agents. His buddies or father would come down to the station and pay a bribe, and he would be released several days later. Now, in Tehran, the city cops were also feared because they are very unprofessional and violent.

Reliving another arrest by city cops, Reza remembered being arrested and handcuffed to 20 or so other prisoners rounded up during one of the many staged propaganda set-ups the regime showed on TV. The purpose was to make the general public believe the police were doing a good job. The corrupt police chief would order a sweep of anyone who even looks like a bad guy, and cuff them together in one long chain link. A television camera would be there to film it all, and a reporter would go to the prisoners and ask them humiliating questions. The prisoners would put their heads down so as not to be identified by the cameras.

With a few of his cronies by his side, the police chief stood proud and tall, talking about what a great job his force was doing in combating crime. The reporter would find someone in the community who knows better than to say anything negative or remotely critical about the government or police force for fear of retribution. Once on camera, they would give the rehearsed line on camera about how great the police are and what an amazing job they are doing fighting crime.

Reza recounted being crammed with more than twenty men into a van made to fit eight. The police drove to their destination, the parking lot of a detention center. One of the police officers unloaded two cans of CS gas in the crowded van and then quickly shut the door and windows so the prisoners would feel the full impact of both cans. The prisoners were crushing each other with their body weight and handcuffs, trying to find relief from the CS gas. As a young Marine, I was exposed to CS gas as a part of my training. I remembered the burning in the throat, lungs, and nostrils, along with the enormous amount of mucus and saliva it produced as you struggled to breathe. I could only imagine what it was like for these 20 men picked at random for a propaganda arrest.

Thirty minutes later, the sliding door of the van opened, and the prisoners stumbled over one another to get out. When they did finally escape to the fresh air, baton strikes were waiting for them. The hits came from every direction. City cops liked to practice their baton strikes on these "hoodlums." While criminals are looked negatively upon anywhere in the world, in Iran, the government has portrayed them as subhuman. In an attempt to deflect the governments' failures and to hide the fact that the biggest cause of crime is due to corrupt policies and economic inequality, they use these "arrests" to make the case that crime existed because these few hoodlums have strayed from the teachings of Islam. They never mention the socioeconomic reasons behind these crimes, only that they were acts committed by deviant creatures who were evil and enjoyed committing them.

Reza said that while getting beaten with the batons, they were pulled, pushed, and grabbed by the cops. Still in their handcuffs, they were dragged into the detention center, and thrown inside a small holding cell. The cell had nothing inside of it. They were held here for days, sometimes weeks. During the first few days, most of the cases were resolved as the families of these young men would come, and pay the piper and offer the right official the right bribe. Those that did not have a family would stay behind, and get beaten. Once a day, the city police officers would have them stick their unwashed hands between the bars. They would dump food in their hands, and the prisoners lapped it up like a dog because handcuffs still bound their hands together. Their bed was the cold, concrete floor of the cell. They did not receive blankets. The prisoners were allowed a total of two bathroom breaks a day. The slightest irritation by the prisoners would induce a baton beating from the cops running the detention center.

Prisoners would come, and prisoners would go. Sometimes the holding cell would be filled with addicts who, in withdrawal, would defecate and vomit all over themselves. At night, the cell would fill with cimex lectularius, better known as bed bugs. I would come to know these creatures very well while I was imprisoned in Evin because they were everywhere there. They only come out at night to suck on your blood and leave a 3-point mark that stings and then continues to itch for days. Each time we would catch one, we'd see its dark red color from the blood it stole from us the night before.

Reza said he was forced to confess to over 20 thefts that had happened over the last year in one neighborhood. Residents reported the thefts but they were never solved. Rather than do police work and solve the crime, the city cops packaged a high number of crimes together and pinned it on one unfortunate individual. This individual would then be put on the TV while the police chief commended his police force for their amazing work in bringing down this criminal mastermind – an illiterate, 24-year-old, crystal meth addict.

Despite the horrific treatment by the city cops, Reza surprised me when, at the end of the story, he said he would rather spend a year in the city detention center than do another 41 days in solitary confinement at Evin. He tried to bargain with the prison guards and told them that they could beat him every day if they would just let him out of solitary confinement, even if just to clean toilets. I had spent eight months in the isolation of solitary confinement. I understand what he meant. I couldn't help but wonder how he would cope, though, if he had been me.

Chapter Thirteen
The Judge of Death and The Deceiver

A few days after Iran's Revolutionary Guard Corps (IRGC) claimed to have downed a US Drone, the RQ-170, Iran's Ministry of Intelligence and Security, in direct competition with the IRGC, claimed to have made a catch of their own. For two days, the MOIS teased this breaking news on television and print without detail. And then, finally, they released a documentary called "Caught." "Caught," told the story of how the MOIS tracked a trained CIA spy who infiltrated Iran through Afghanistan and showed a man confessing to these actions on television. That man was me.

Mohsen Rezaee, a former high-ranking IRGC official and owner of an Iranian news site called Tabnak, claimed that I had infiltrated Iran to rescue the RQ-170. The MOIS claimed that I was arrested in December and confessed almost the same day that the video played on Iranian state television. Only after I went to the political prison did I learn more about the rivalry between MOIS, and IRGC from other inmates - some of whom worked previously for both organizations. In the MOIS version, I was spotted immediately after my arrival at the airport by intelligence agents, and they quickly were able to out me as a CIA spy. Conveniently leaving out the fact that I had been tortured, and held in solitary confinement for many months. Iran controlled the narrative, and their propaganda was telling the world that I was a CIA spy, and had been caught due to the prowess of the country's security services.

In their documentary, there I was, dressed well with a luxury hotel in the background. I'm clean-shaven and had the buzz of nicotine in my system. They showed pictures of me from my days in the military that they had taken from my cellphone and laptop. The video said that these were taken by Iranian agents who had been tracking me even though I was smiling in them, and they were clearly pictures that I was aware were being taken. Other pictures taken from my Facebook account showed a more relaxed me. MOIS – a controlling arm of the media – sentenced me in the press by putting this video out before I ever went to any court. I hadn't even spoken to a lawyer. Besides guards and interrogators, I hadn't spoken to anyone at all.

Several days later, I was raced into Iran's Revolutionary Court early in the morning. Looking rough and scruffy and in my prison uniform, I entered the office of a man internationally nicknamed, "The Butcher" and every other curse word in Iranian vocabulary. Judge Abolghassem Salavati is a man that controversy follows and is known for his harsh sentences – including many death sentences – of human rights activists, journalists, political prisoners, and peaceful demonstrators. Salavati is also the preferred judge of the IRGC and MOIS because he doesn't do his duty as a judge but rather takes orders directly from these two organizations. For his actions, in December of 2019, the U.S. Department of the Treasury placed economic sanctions against him.

The guards took me directly to his office. He spoke to me casually, like I was an old buddy that had walked into his office for a friendly visit. He had his tea boy offer me a small tea with sugar cubes.

"Look, Amir, you're a good kid, and I want to help you. There are a few cameras in the courtroom today. Just cooperate with us. This is political, you know. Say you made a mistake, say the Americans fooled you. I'll help you."

Judge Salavati rarely spoke to the prisoner, nor did he invite them in his personal office and offer them tea. Just as I was digesting what he was saying and about to sip my tea, a colorful man walked in and shook Judge Salavati's hand, kissing him on each cheek. These two were very good friends.

After their embrace with a half chuckle, Judge Salavati smiles at me and points to the man who entered and said, "And this is your court-appointed lawyer."

"Look, Amir," the man said as he sat next to me, "The evidence is stacked against you, and I can think of no defense. I reviewed your file. I am the only lawyer who can do so, and it is clear that you are guilty. You confessed."

After this motivational speech and deliverance of hope by my corrupt court-appointed lawyer who didn't even try to hide the fact that he was a servant of Judge Salavati, I was speechless. Iran is a country where its people in power talked about religion and justice that none of them actually believed. In their so-called Revolutionary Court, they could say or do anything with impunity and play with people's lives. They handed out harsh sentences and the death penalty like candy handed out on Halloween. It is all done in the name of the Revolution.

The prosecutor had a perfectly logical explanation for this. He said, "Do you think we will give the revolution to the judges?" Meaning that the intelligence, and security service are the ones who deserve absolute power in the country. This man walked with a clear arrogance and talked with a sense of entitlement I had never seen before. He gave himself enormous credit for bringing about the revolution and looked upon Iran as his dominion. The judges, the people, all just subjects that should be thankful they can live in his realm. This sort of blanket authority granted to these groups by the Supreme Leader in exchange for their loyalty is the cause of the massive corruption and human rights abuses throughout the country. It is also why billions of dollars have gone unaccounted for inside Iran at the people's expense.

I was ushered out of Salavati's office and into the courtroom, where press photographers took photos of me in my prison uniform while my lawyer told the cameras how America had tricked me. I deserved Islamic leniency. Twenty minutes later, I was whisked away again and taken back to my cell to await my sentence. I didn't even know what happened. It was a trial – Iranian-style.

In my vulnerable state, I hoped that Judge Salavati would follow through on the promises he made to me in his office to help me and that this nightmare would be over soon. After what I experienced in Salavati's office, I drew the conclusion that all they wanted to do was to trick me, release a video, and get the propaganda win. They would tell the world that America even tricks its citizens, and they would show the world how compassionate Iran is by setting me free.

Two weeks later, a guard had passed by and mumbled something to me about keeping my faith in God. That evening I was summoned and taken to an interrogation room. A small television sat on the table in front of me. Shortly after, Haji entered and turned on the television. Next to the bright red "Breaking News" graphic was a picture of me with my scruffy beard in my prison uniform. I couldn't believe how pale, weak, and skinny I was. I looked horrible. There were no mirrors in Ward 209 so this was the first time I was able to see myself.

"Hekmati is sentenced to death by hanging by Judge Salavati in Branch 15 of the Islamic Republic of Iran's Revolutionary Court."

WHAT?!? I was trying to process what I just saw. I couldn't believe it. My chest tightened, and my breathing became shallow. Death. By. Hanging. Death. DEATH! No, no, this cannot be true. I thought this was another one of the little games they were playing with me.

They wanted something more from me. It wasn't real. It was a false video that Haji created as another form of torture – white torture – the kind that leaves scars on your mind, not your body.

Haji then slammed a newspaper on the table. It was the Keyhan, one of Iran's most-read papers, and there I was on the front page in my military uniform. I was famous in Iran because now everyone in Iran knew that I, Amir Hekmati, a US Marine Veteran and American citizen, was to be executed my hanging sometime – any time – soon.

"Have I killed somebody?" I shouted, "I did everything you demanded! You said this was going to get me released, that I would return to my family, and now you want to kill me?!"

"Take him!" Haji half chuckles and half yells. This man was truly evil. I scuffled with the guards when they came to gather me, and they slammed me up against the wall.

Haji came in close and spoke in my ear, "Don't worry, Amir. If you are innocent, you will be a martyr and go to heaven. If you are guilty, then being executed will rid you of your sins, and again you will go to heaven, so there is no worry."

It took me a few seconds to digest what this madman was saying. I paused to see if this was more cruelty from him or if this was a sincere thought. It was a sincere thought. He was serious. I wondered where this type of thought might have come from and believe that this is what his bosses tell him so that he doesn't have to feel guilty for the horrible things he does to people every day. They tell these guys that either way, the men they abuse, torment, and kill are going to heaven, so they are doing them a favor. This is how the regime justifies the terrible things they do to ordinary people.

"You worry about where you are going, you bastard! Either way, I'm going to heaven, and you're going straight to hell, you piece of shit!" I shouted at him as the guards were rushing me away from the room and back to my cell.

Once inside, I crumbled into myself in the corner. I thought about my parents. I thought about my sisters and brother. All of the things that were important to me started flooding my thoughts. Then I felt anguish, especially when I thought of the pain my mother must have been feeling. If it were on the news in Iran, it wouldn't be long before my mother heard from relatives about what they would see on television. Then I pictured my death. I pictured walking up steps, a blindfold being placed around my eyes, a rope around my neck. I wondered if my neck would break on impact, and it would be a quick death or if my life would slowly and painfully drain away from me. I imagined my mother when the news of my execution reached her. I pictured her forced to come to Iran to claim my body at the morgue to discover my neck, black as night from having the life pulled out of me. I started packing my mental luggage for the next world.

After wrestling with the guilt I felt for the pain I know my family would be living through, I started to find some comfort in the thought of death. I wouldn't have to live like this anymore. I wouldn't randomly have dirty water thrown on me to deprive me of sleep. I wouldn't have to answer any more questions. I wouldn't feel the weight of the batons beat down on me anymore. I wouldn't have to see Haji and be taunted by his evil and his freedom. I wouldn't be alone with my thoughts all the time in this small cell.

I began to bargain with myself and with God. I promised us both that if I somehow made it out of this, I would focus on those things that were occupying my mind right now. I would remember to tell the people I love that I loved them. I would take care of my mother and father, my sisters, and my brother. I would be a fantastic, fun uncle. I would continue to seek knowledge. I would remember the things every day that bring me joy and be grateful for them. I would seek a peaceful mind, calm heart, and a spirit that sought not only to be good but to do good, too. I started to have regrets. There was a girl back home I cared for, and we were close. Why didn't I ever tell her how I felt? I thought of my days growing up and being care-free, able to go where I wanted, and do whatever it was that I wanted to do. Why didn't I ever appreciate that I could be care-free? I began negotiations with the almighty debating with him the good that could be gained from sparing me at 28 years old.

I began picturing people in a crowded mall or a street. They were above, walking, and I was below them in the sewers, slowly dying. They freely walked about, laughing, while I was below them swimming in misery and pain. Did they know about the prisoners here buried alive under a mountain of oppression as they went about their daily lives until they made the wrong person mad or until someone could gain something from locking them away? As they stressed over trivial things that do not matter, I just wanted to be able to see a bird. There was a pigeon that had a nest somewhere behind a vent in the top corner of my cell, whenever it would land, I would talk to it and give it messages to pass to the outside. This was my version of email – pigeon mail – only I could never see the bird, so I never received a reply.

I became even more vigilant. I never knew when the execution would happen. Each time the guards would drop off my meals, I would become terrified, thinking that this was it. They'd cuff me, march me up the ladder, and kick the ladder from under me. I tried to shield my startled state from the guards, but I didn't do very well at times. Even now, when doors open suddenly, my chest fills with pressure, and I need to tell myself that everything is ok. As I said, white torture leaves scars on your mind, and those scars are meant to stay with you.

Eventually, I wore myself out from the continual activation of my fight or flight instinct. My body started to resist to save energy. I became detached from who I was, where I was, what I was, and the outside world. I again reached the point that I didn't care what happened. Time, ambition, goals, the future, death – all of the things we stress about in our daily lives became nothing. Less than nothing. I was content to be released back in the world, live in a tent on a beach, hunt for my dinner, and live in peace. In solitary, this is my highest ambition.

Time began to move forward, and I lived this daily death march each day. I still had not been allowed visits from my family in Iran or to call my family at home in Michigan. My thoughts went to dark places. Since my experience, I've come to believe that extended punishments and prison sentences do not rehabilitate, but they only make one more accepting of violence and violent behavior. You feel like the world does not have a drop of mercy for you, so why should you feel mercy for it?

Prison can destroy your moral fabric if you allow it. Luckily, I had my beliefs in God and prayer. Prayer was elusive for me during this time though, and my beliefs were tested. There were times when I didn't know what the point of praying was anymore. Other times, I felt betrayed by God. After I would pray though, I would feel better. Secure. Calm. It was like I was inside the bare framing of a house, and with each prayer, a brick was laid to strengthen me and give me exterior protection from the onslaught of worry that surrounded me.

****

A few days later, I am forced into the interrogation room where Haji is waiting. I wasn't sure what the point of these conversations was anymore. He quickly showed me.

"How do you feel?" Haji smugly asked me.

"I've been sentenced to death by hanging. How do you think I feel?!"

"We are working on getting a sentence reduction, Amir, but you have to help us. We don't control the court; we can only make a recommendation. The truth is you are abandoned."

"The United States Government, your family, lawyers - no one else can help you. Right now, I can help you. You need to think about yourself, Amir. You were a Marine, you served in the US Military, and now you are abandoned. In a few days, we will execute you unless you help yourself. We have a camera waiting. We want you to tell the President of the United States and the people of America how frustrated you are for being left to die. We are not out to harm you, Amir, this is between our governments, but it's up to you. I don't care either way."

This man was unbelievable. He has lied to me so many times already. This man did nothing but lie. I wouldn't play along anymore. I couldn't. I felt humiliated for being tricked and felt horrible that I helped Iran push out propaganda against the United States. Enough is enough, and I have had more than my fair share of enough.

"Do whatever you want. If you want to execute me, go ahead. If you have something to say to the US government, say it yourself. Not through me as your puppet. Or maybe it's you that is scared?"

"Take him back to his cell!" Haji yells to the guards. They rush in to take me back to my cell again.

*****

A month had gone by when I was suddenly told to step out of my cell. This was it, the time had come, and my 28 years on this earth were coming to a sad, and horrific end. I didn't want to scuffle with the guards. I didn't want to plead. I didn't want to give them that satisfaction, so I feigned calm. With the blindfold on, I'm resigned to deep sadness. This was it. Each time the blindfold was lowered, it was dreadful. This time was different, though, the darkness I was experiencing was like the eternal darkness I would face soon. I thought about my corpse lying in the dirt as my flesh began to rot. Along with sadness, I felt relief. I was tired. I would no longer have to suffer. Instead of heading to the gallows, to my surprise, we headed towards the gates leading outside of the prison. Once outside the prison, the agent told me that I could remove my blindfold, and I do so gladly. I'm confused. Then it hit me. They were going to take me to the middle of Tehran and hang me from a crane somewhere

where people had already gathered, and my execution would be public. Iran is a propaganda state, and what better propaganda than to hang any American publicly in Tehran for the world to see.

Chapter Fourteen
Mother

Several minutes later, we didn't pull up to my public execution, but to the Revolutionary Court, the same building where I had met Judge Salavati. I ask the guards why we were there, and they didn't answer. And then I see a familiar face. Mom? Is that really you?

The agent squeezed the hand that is around my arm and tells me that I am to tell my mother that I'm good and that everything is fine, or else they will punish me by cutting our meeting short. My mom looked like she had aged ten years since the last time I saw her six or seven months ago. While I had no tears left to shed from my eyes, inside, I was sobbing. I knew telling her what had happened to me here would do no good. She had been through enough. I wanted to have every precious moment with her that I could, and I wasn't willing to risk losing this time with her. I nod my head at the agent, signaling I got the message. He waves a guard to take me into the small room next to the courtroom that has been set up for us to visit.

As is mandatory in Iran, my mother was wearing a long-sleeved blouse and scarf. I couldn't help but think that her choice in color of both - black - was her subtle way of saying just what she thought of this whole situation - it was like death. She walked fast towards me with a face full of worry and a napkin in her hand that she used to wipe away any tears that may fall. In the room, I noticed that there was a glass divider with a newspaper taped over it. I knew that this was likely where Haji was sitting on the other side to listen in on my conversation.

Once inside, we sit down across from each other with the agent that provided me the warning only moments ago sitting between us. In ordinary circumstances, this would be uncomfortable, but we were so happy to see each other that we hardly noticed he was there. At that moment, I was so impressed with my mother and her strength. I could see she was visibly holding back her tears and trying to act calm because she knew that if she broke down, it would hurt me too. She provided me with peace and calm, something I hadn't had in months. She provided me with something new. Hope. Everything she said was so positive and encouraging. For the first time, I learned about the support I had outside of the walls of Evin Prison. I learned that people all over the world were calling for my release.

She told me that lawyers in America and Iran were working on my case and that the United States government was involved as well. For the first time since three men showed up at my uncle's house and told me I needed to come with them, I didn't feel alone. I began to think about what she was saying. If the world was talking about my unjust imprisonment, would Iran execute me? She tried to give me more details, but the agent stopped her. It was obvious that the agents had had a similar talk with her as they had with me. Frustrated, my mom gave the agent a dirty look and said, "Don't worry, Amir, Jaan, the whole world is following your case!"

For ten minutes, my mother has tried to get more information from me about my treatment and I kept deflecting her questions. I didn't want to tell my mother anything that could put her at risk. I was worried they might prevent her from leaving Iran and going back to America. They would be worried she would return to the United States and tell the world of the horrors of my treatment, and they would want to avoid the bad press. I knew my mom would understand the things I didn't say as much as the things I did. Mothers have a sixth sense when it comes to their children, especially when their children are lying or trying to cover something up. While I told my mother that I was feeling great and there was nothing to worry about, she could see by my mannerisms, my appearance, and my weight loss that wasn't true. I could tell that the weight loss was especially hard for her by the way she kept looking at me. She covered up her anger at seeing the shape I was in with awkward smiles and uncomfortable pauses.

The agent informed us we had five minutes left for our visit. As our visit was coming to an end, I could see my mother getting agitated with the agent sitting between us. I did my best to keep her calm by maintaining eye contact, asking her questions, and trying to make fun of the situation. My mother and I shared an emotional hug. Holding my mom close opened up all the wounds I had tried to keep closed during our visit. It reminded me of the world I was deprived of and the world I was now living in.

Guards escorted me into a courtroom, where an Imam was wearing a turban, and two men in suits were sitting behind a desk. They prevented my mother from entering the office.

"Don't worry," an agent said with a smirk on his face, "he's a good boy. We will take care of him."

My mother is unable to hold back her anger. "Your turn is coming! One day, you will be the one being judged!"

⸻

Chapter 15:

The Appeal

The room I entered was not a courtroom, as I had thought, but was the personal office of Judge Mohammad Moghiseh of the Revolutionary Court, Branch 28. Like Judge Salavati, Mohammad Moghiseh has a reputation for his disdain of human rights activists, journalists, political prisoners, and peaceful protesters and is known for giving out the harshest sentences from the shortest trials. The EU has placed sanctions on him for his lawlessness, and, like Salavati, the US Treasury placed economic sanctions against him in 2019. Unlike Judge Salavati, Mohammad Moghiseh was a cleric or Imam. The man sitting to the right of Judge Moghiseh was his secretary and notetaker, and the man on this left was an intelligence agent, or the puppet master because he was the one who would determine what happened to me next.

The judge's assistant showed me to a chair while the Imam stared me down. The intelligence agent was talking quietly and quickly into the judge's ear. Judge Moghiseh nodded and continued to stare at me. He nodded again. He continued to stare. The intelligence agent gave the cleric further instructions in his ear. The secretary looked at me and smirked. That's when I realized this was a type of trial – perhaps a formality before they executed me. The agent calls someone on his cellphone, puts the phone on speaker, and sets it on the desk. I'm certain he has called Haji so the bastard can listen in.

"State your name," the judge says, finally breaking his silence. "Amir Hekmati."

Barely able to hear me, he motions for one of the guards in the room to put a chair in front of his desk so he could hear me better. I sit down closer and am now face-to-face with all three men. The intelligence agent on the left is looking at me with contempt like he is angry that they haven't executed me yet. The judge looks at me confused and reads a document in front of him.

"Tell me why you entered Iran, what you were planning on spying on, and what your orders were from the CIA."

I was finally getting the opportunity to speak on my behalf. "CIA! This was my first time in Iran, ever. I was with my family the entire time I was here, and they can attest to that. I had no orders from anyone. I saw my family, ate at a few restaurants, spent time with my uncle. What exactly could I do, and when?"

Judge Moghiseh exchanged looks with the intelligence agent. He is annoyed as he asks me his second question, "What did you do in the military?"

"I explained this to the Iranian Interests section when I applied for a visa. I was 17 when I joined the US military. That was ten years ago. It had nothing to do with Iran. I left the military when I was 22. That was five years before I traveled to Iran."

Again, the Judge looked confused, and the agent leaned over and whispered in his ear. He nodded and told his assistant to write down that I admitted to being in the United States military. I couldn't believe how this was being handled. There was no transcriber or translator, and out of all the points I had made as to why my military service was irrelevant, there was no record taken of my defense. The judge was taking orders from the intelligence agent that he would then order his assistant to carry out.

"And did you learn how to use a weapon in the military?" he asked.

"Yes, I never had any weapons in Iran. Am I being charged with using a weapon?" I asked.

The judge says to his scribe, "Write down that he admits to having received lethal training."

"Were you involved in combat operations in Iraq?"

"Yes, and I'm proud to have served my country, the United States, there." I realized this is another show trial, so I was going to give answers that made me at least made me feel good about who I was and how I had lived my life.

The judge barks at his scribe this time in a voice he thinks will scare and intimidate me. " "Write down that he admits to having used weapons previously in a neighboring Muslim country, and has received lethal military training."

The intelligence agent looks satisfied. They whispered among themselves, and then I was taken outside the room. As I'm leaving, I search the hallways to see if I can find my mother and get one last glimpse of her. I don't know the next time I will be able to see her. I don't know if I will be alive to see her again.

*****

Nearly two months later, a guard gathers me and leads me down a few halls to where an older man is waiting with a bunch of papers in his hand.

"Name?" he asks.

"Amir Hekmati," I reply.

He shuffled through his papers until he found what he was looking for and places a piece of paper in front of me. I began reading when he tells me to hurry up and sign. When I asked what it was, he again told me to hurry up and sign it. I can see that it is a new charge sheet.

Amir Hekmati admits to military service in the United States.

Amir Hekmati admits to receiving military training from the United States.

Amir Hekmati admits to serving in Iraq with the US military.

Sentence: 10 years of Prison for 'Cooperating with a hostile entity: The CIA"

Everything that Judge Moghiseh had told his assistant to write down was here in front of me on this paper that this man was expecting me to sign as if he was dropping off a pizza delivery. With this paper, I knew one thing for sure: Iran had realized that whatever they had hoped to accomplish by sentencing me to death had been futile. With this paper in front of me, I knew that I had escaped death.

It would be two years after the overturning of my death sentence for my retrial to happen.

My trial happened in a secret, closed-door meeting that I received no notification of and where my lawyer, an Iranian attorney my family hired to represent me, was not present to offer a defense on my behalf. I went from convicted of being an Enemy of God, the harshest crime in Iran that meted out the harshest punishment – death – to someone who cooperated with a hostile country, my own. They used the answers to the questions I was asked that day in Judge Moghiseh's private office to convict me. My "cooperation" was my military service in defense of the country I was born in, the USA.

Chapter Sixteen
Rebellion

Handing me that paper to sign was handing me information, and that information provided me with perspective. I didn't have a death sentence. I didn't have a sentence at all. I would be waiting here until the powers that be in Iran decided they had exhausted my usefulness, and then I would be released. I was a political prisoner – a hostage, really – and whenever the ransom was paid, whatever that price would be, I would go home. My focus had to change from worrying if I had a future to worry about now. I still had a very difficult challenge ahead, but the worst was behind me, and it was just a matter of time.

They began letting me go outside every three days to walk around a secure area that had high walls, cameras watching me, and no room. It was not a big yard, but large enough that I could do a light jog in a circle while wearing my cheap, plastic shower sandals. I was finally able to show every three days, but these days didn't coincide, so I would have to live in my sweat until show day. I couldn't resist getting my heart rate up and working out some of the stress and pain in my body, so I ran like hell each time. The plastic sandals made running difficult, so I would throw them off and run barefoot.

My running really pissed off the guards because it showed them that I still had strength and motivation despite everything they had done to try to break me. Emboldened, and angry as hell at my situation I started yelling Marine Corps cadence on one day while in the small yard.

"C-130 going down the strip! US Marines are gonna take a little trip! Stand up, buckle up, shuffle to the door! Jump right out and shout Marine Corps!"

Over, and over again as I ran in circles in my prison pajamas, and plastic sandals. As loud as I could get, and Marines were known for being able to project their voice. Not even a minute later, and I was yelled at by the guard once to shut up, but I pretended like I couldn't hear him. I started to run faster and scream the cadence at the top of my lungs. It didn't take long for several guards to run into the yard with their batons drawn. I kept running in circles and pretended that I didn't see them. Then they started to chase me until they managed to cut me off, and I was blocked. They weren't there to make me stop singing. They were there to dole out a beating. I had been the target of their batons so many times by this time that I knew what was coming. I tried to block my face and vitals, and their batons found my body with force.

Once they had beaten me to the ground, the head guard at the door signaled to them to stop.

They gathered me up and threw me in the cell. I wouldn't get another yard break for a very long time.

One morning after breakfast, I was surprised to hear the guards heading towards my door outside of their normal routine. The hatch opened. A guard looked around and then abruptly left. A few minutes later, I heard him come back. Standing behind him is another prisoner holding his blankets in hand, with his blindfold on, standing hunched over and uneasy. The guard pushed the prisoner into my very small cell. I don't know what this is about or who the hell this person is. The prisoner stood still with his blindfold on. After a minute of uneasy silence, I say hello and startle him. Confused, and amused by this lost rookie detainee I decided to have a little fun. I'd pretend to be an interrogator, and see what would happen. I figured he had no idea what room he was just placed in, and he was facing the wall, holding his blankers, blindfold securely fastened.

"Are you ready to cooperate and tell me what you did?" I asked. "I didn't do anything. I swear!" the man cries out.

I chuckled inside at first, but then immediately felt bad. I knew what this felt like, and didn't want to be one of them. I placed my hand on the man's shoulder and told him to calm down. He moved away from me and blocked his face to protect it from incoming blows. By his reaction, it was obvious that this prisoner had been beaten and abused by his interrogator. I reached for the blindfold and pulled it off so he could see me and see that I was in the same prison uniform he wore. The prisoner was shocked and looked around the room in astonishment. It took him a few moments to calm down. We talked, and after a few hours he realized who I was. He told me he had seen my confession and news of my conviction on Iranian state television. He sympathized with me and told me he hadn't believed any of it. I was worried about giving personal information to him, but I figured I had nothing to lose. I asked him to memorize my sister's phone number and to call her when he was released and let her know I was ok. He did so hesitantly. The next day he was removed from my cell. I suspect that our conversation had been monitored.

There were other ways I tried to get news out to my family. Visits and phone calls were still denied to me — no contact with anyone but the guards and my interrogators. I wasn't even permitted to read newspapers, even though many other detainees were at the time. We were occasionally given a small yogurt cup with a peel-off aluminum lid to mix in with our rice at lunch. I discovered that if I rolled the aluminum yogurt lid and pressed it against a wall, it would write. The lid would leave a thin grey mark against the wall that I could use to write small letters. I planned to use it to write my name on the bathroom wall.

In Ward 209, there are no toilets in the room, so to go to the bathroom, you had to press a button in the cell and wait for the guard to open the door and take you to the toilets. With the blindfold on, you would walk down the hall past other cells to use the bathroom and then walk back. In the bathroom, however, the door was closed, and you had some privacy. I'd write a message on the wall and see if I get a response from another inmate. The first time, I wrote my first name – Amir. Amir is a common name, so if the guards saw it, I could deny it. I did receive a reply from someone who signed his name as Mohsen. Mohsen said that he would get a message out for me. A guard came later that day to give a stern warning. They had small peephole cameras in the bathroom, as well. So much for a few moments of privacy.

My cell was the farthest from the bathroom so I had to pass 5 or 6 cells with my blindfold on when walking to the bathroom. Sometimes the guard would see my light on and walk to my cell door open it, and then walk back to the end of the hall where a camera, and the guard sat and watched one prisoner at a time walk to the bathroom, leave, and walk back to his cell and close his cell door which locked behind him. The guard would then walk to the cell door, confirm the door was locked, get eyes on you, and walk away. That is how you would go to the bathroom. Once in a while prisoners would whisper things as I walked by to go to the bathroom. With my blindfold on I could only hear little whispers, so it kind of freaked me out. Most of the time the guards would take their sweet time to open the door. You could hit the light, but maybe wait 30 minutes, 1 hour, 2 hours, there was no pattern to when the guard would finally come, and open your door. You needed a bladder of steel to avoid soiling yourself in Ward 209. A new arrival, an older man was down the hall in a cell, and either didn't know about the light system, or was confused why the guard was taking so long to open the door and let him go to the bathroom. The prisoner gets frustrated and calls out to the guard. "Guard! Guard!" Bored, and amused by this I respond to him from behind my cell door a few cells down from him, pretending to be a guard. "Yeah! What is it!" I reply. "I need to go!" the man replies. "Forget it, in an hour!" I respond. "But I really need to go!" the man replies. I feel bad for him, but I am cracking up. We go back, and forth and the man is really yelling at who he thinks is a guard, pleading to go potty. 20 minutes or so, a guard creeps up, and pops in front of my cell. I shrug, and walk towards the back of my cell startled. We make eye contact, and I can tell that the guard is trying to hold back his laughter. He says with a half-smile, "Don't do that again!" I nod ok, and take a seat against the wall. The prisoner is finally let out, and I can hear him racing for the bathroom. My mischief came abruptly to an end, and I was back to sitting in my cell passing time.

*****

Life in Ward 209 went on, everyday a battle for survival. No yard, no exercise, no proper food, no telephone calls, no visits, no newspapers, no books, no tv, nothing!I had endured beatings, torture, and a death sentence. I was starting to hit a new emotional low. I began to argue with the head of Ward 209 that since they were using me as a political pawn, I should go to the political prison.

I decided that I would go on a hunger strike. I had arguments with the guards every day as the balance of power became more uneven with each day I spent in that solitary cell. I knew that my real power was that they wanted me alive so they could use me as a bargaining chip. I knew now that they were never going to execute me. They thought they could scare the US government and attract attention by issuing the death penalty. They lost credibility when two months later, they annulled the sentence due to insufficient evidence. No, they wanted me alive and well to ensure they could bargain for me. They didn't want the word to get out about how they had treated me, tricked me into the confession, and that I was innocent of everything they said I was. If I could go on a hunger strike long enough to make them worried about my health, they might make some concessions to me. Maybe I would get a phone call, a visit, or get moved to the political prison where I could have the same privileges as other prisoners. I was in a detention center inside the prison. My situation was so dire that I was begging to be sent to a normal prison where inmates had access to basics and rights that were denied to me. After all I had suffered, being hungry would not be a problem. I was ready to do anything to cause problems for them. I had nothing to lose.

The next morning, when the guard opened my door to give me my piece of stale bread and little packets of butter and jam, I threw them on the floor and stomped on them and then threw them again, this time out my door. The guard slammed the door and walked off, pissed as hell at my act of rebellion. Ordinarily, a prisoner would take a severe beating for this kind of outburst, but they didn't come back until lunch. At lunch, I told the guard to take the food and dump it over his head. I informed him that I was on a hunger strike and would continue until they gave me a phone call and sent me to the political prison. He returned a short time later and told me to put my blindfold. I didn't know what to expect. Maybe they were going to give me my phone call, or maybe they were going to tie me down and shovel food into my mouth.

Instead, I'm led down the hall to a man wearing a suit. I have my blindfold on and can only see his polished shoes. I don't recognize his voice. I have no idea who he is.

"Hi Amir, what's the problem?"

"A year and a half in a hole is the problem. No phone. No visits. No Exercise. Am I a human being?" I barked at him.

"Calm down, Amir," he said in a thin voice, "I know it's hard. We'll talk with Haji and see if we can take you to the yard more often but forget the phone call. You need to stay put for now. Come now, Amir, eat your food. What are you - a kid? You're only going to hurt yourself."

"I'm sorry, I don't have anything else to lose. Do you think I'm bluffing? I'm going all the way. No phone, no food."

I turned around and walked back to my cell. Several hours later, dinner arrives. "Not eating!" The guard closed the door and walked away. I go to sleep a little hungry that night, but the hope of getting a phone call and hearing my family's voice and knowing that they are ok gives me strength. The next morning, they brought my breakfast, "Not eating!" I continued this for three days until the guard called me out again, and the man with the polished shoes pleads with me again to eat — two more days without food pass. I remembered hearing you can go thirty days or more without food, but you needed water which I had. I was on day five. I would keep going.

Going on a hunger strike is probably one of the most difficult things anyone can do. You are fighting your body's most basic instincts. There was nothing to do, nothing to look forward to. I didn't realize how much I counted on those meals to occupy my day. I started feeling weak. I spent my days lying down and staring at the ceiling. I had no energy. I couldn't be bothered to talk. I could hardly move. I would keep going.

It was now winter, and our insulation in the cell was a thin sheet of plastic. The cell was freezing. It felt like being in a morgue. We had three military blankets, the same ones I had in boot camp as a Marine. One would be placed on the floor to sleep on, the second folded into a small pillow, and the third used to cover yourself. It was so cold that I took the second blanket and put it on top of me, so I had no pillow. I would go completely under the blanket to shield myself from the cold and trap the heat of my body. If we were lucky, a little sun would come out the next morning, and the weather would warm up a little bit. One night, while under the blankets, I needed to use the restroom. It was freezing. All I remember was standing up, and everything went black. When I came to again, deeply confused, I heard a guard yelling from the hatch. I had passed out. My head was throbbing, so I must have banged it on the hard floor when I went unconscious. The guard didn't come in to help. He continued to yell through the hatch. I slowly rolled over and crawled to the wall where I could sit up and have my back supported. I sat there in a daze.

A few hours later, two guards came. They told me to get up because we needed to see the doctor. I crept up slowly, using the wall to assist me. My energy level was so low. The doctor was worried that I had gotten a brain injury from my fall. He asked me to put my finger on my nose while I stood on one foot. It reminded me of a sobriety test. He asked a few questions about my health, took my blood pressure, and looked a little concerned with the results. Of course, he didn't express any of this to me.

Later that night, several guards came and stood outside my cell. I was told to grab my blankets, put on my blindfold, and step out. I had no idea what was going on. In the hall with my blindfold on and blankets in hand, the man with the polished shoes walked up to me.

"You said you wanted to go to the prison, right?" he said. "Yes"

"You got your wish. Don't let them eat you alive over there." He said.

"Let's hope I don't eat them," I respond. Polished Shoes chuckled and motions the guards to take me away.

☒

Part Three
Ward 350

Chapter Seventeen:
Welcome to Evin University

I drop off my blankets in a laundry room and am led into an examination room. I'm forced to strip, squat, cough to make sure that I have no other prisoner's information written down anywhere. Then I'm handed the clothes that I had on when the intelligence agents took me from my uncle's home. It felt great to put them on even though they sagged on me because I had lost so much weight. I felt like a person again in my clothes. I'm blindfolded again as we walk through the detention center's maze. I hear locks turning and doors being popped open. We step outside, and the fresh air hits me. I take in several deep breaths. It feels so good to breathe in the fresh air. We reached the security gate that slowly opened. Once on the other side of the gate, a prison guard in a military uniform becomes my guide. He tells me to take my blindfold off. I look back and see the backs of the guards.

My new guard takes me to in-processing for the prison. They take my photo, and I'm fingerprinted. After all this time in the detention center of the MOIS, I am now officially being processed into Evin prison. Until this moment, I had been a ghost. After being in-processed, I walk with the guard to find my new home and see the sprawling prison complex for the first time. The guard is interested in who I am and tried to start a conversation with me. He had a paper with my picture on it. The paper also listed my sentence and the description of my crime: "Cooperation with the CIA Against the

Islamic Republic of Iran." He knew he was taking me to the security ward where the special-status prisoners were housed.

The guard and I approach a building that says Ward 3 on it, and after showing the paper with my photo and sentence to a camera, the door buzzes, and we enter. Ward 3 is a building within the Evin Prison complex. There are different sections within the ward. I have no idea where we are going when we finally reach the guards who run Ward 350. After being searched by this new set of guards, I'm searched and given a questionnaire. My escort leaves.

"American?" the new guard asks, "We see you on TV?" I nod.

"Death sentence? Ten years?" he inquires about my fate. "I don't know. It changes all the time".

The guard gave me a puzzled look and motioned me to walk with him over to the entrance door. A massive bolt is pushed back and the heavy steel door opens. Once I walked in, 20 - 30 prisoners all stopped what they were doing to look at me. I still had my huge beard and looked emaciated from my hunger strike, but I knew they recognized me because they began whispering in one another's ears. They had seen me on Iranian TV as the super CIA spy the regime told everyone I was.

The guard passes me off to someone known as the pager. The pager was a prisoner who sat at a desk all day and worked for the guard. Whenever the guard needed someone to be called to his office, he would let the pager know. The pager would call their name over the intercom and have someone fetch the prisoner. The pager got on the intercom and called for Wakeel Band (WB), which literally means lawyer of the ward. He wasn't a lawyer in a legal sense. He's a prisoner viewed as the boss of the prisoners. This designation usually went to the guy who was respected and feared by other prisoners and often had the longest sentence. The WB was supposed to enforce what the guards wanted, and in exchange, the guards would give him and us some autonomy in prison. If the guards wanted to make your life hell for whatever reason, then the WB could intervene and sometimes succeed at getting you a pass. The WB had the best room with two bunks to himself. He also had someone to cook and make tea for him.

Our WB was Hajj Agha Jamalipour. Hajj being an honorific title earned by those that had made the pilgrimage to Mecca to observe the Hajj. Agha was a towering 6'4' with a huge gut. He approached me with a minion on each side while playing with prayer beads in his hand. He began educating me about the ward: what was available, the schedule, the command structure, and an overview of how things worked. If I needed anything, I was to let him know. He instructed one of his men to show me to my cell and dismissed us. I was escorted to my new home, cell 8, where I met my fifteen cellmates. They all stood up, shook my hand, and sat in a circle while they drank tea and asked me questions. They all wore their own street clothes. Prisoners in Ward 350 could have their families bring them approved clothing and, once inspected, taken to the prisoner. A pair of pants, underwear, a couple of shirts. The differences between Ward 209 and Ward 350 were jarring. It was like night and day.

Roll call took place every morning at 7:30 AM and every evening at 5:30 PM. After roll call in the morning, we panned out a thin piece of plastic on the floor. The plastic was our breakfast table. I had gotten adjusted to sitting on the floor in Ward 209. When I was first arrested and stuck in the small solitary cell, there were times it felt like my knees were going to explode. Even today, I can sit in ground positions that were impossible before. The standard Persian breakfast was a little piece of feta cheese, bread, and jam. Sometimes we would have hard-boiled eggs with sweet tea.

Ward 350 was a tough place for most people, but for me, it was heaven. I had already experienced the deepest pits of hell after 18 months in Ward 209, so this felt like an upgrade. Here, I had people I could talk to and things to do. I could buy things, including extra food. There was a small television with state-run channels. I was able to watch the news and feel more connected to the outside world. There was a small yard that I could run in little circles and see the sky every day.

After morning roll call, we were left to our own devices until evening roll call and then left to our own devices again until 10:30 p.m. when lights would go out. There were organized chess games, and I quickly learned who the grandmaster of chess was — a guy named Atlasi. Atlasi was serving a 10-year sentence for working for the CIA. Unlike me, a political pawn that MOIS used for propaganda, Atlasi was the real deal. He was one of many. These men had been recruited, trained, and conducted numerous espionage operations for the CIA, Israeli Mossad, Britain's MI6, and the Mujahedin-e-

Khalq (MEK) organization. There were also a few Al-Qaeda members, Azeri separatists, and people who were part of the Green movement and various other political movements. Some of them were former members of parliament, one man worked for the National Security Council of Iran, and had scaled the US Embassy wall, but had changed his views of the regime and was now serving six years. He served until the very last day of his sentence for refusing to write that he was "sorry." Some of the Al-Qaeda members found out I was former US military, and had served in Iraq, and gave me evil stares. I was on constant alert, most of the Al-Qaeda inmates were on death row, and I could be a target. Relief only came, when they were all transferred to a different prison months later.

Chapter Eighteen
Mohammad Heydari

The first inmate that I began to speak with frequently was Mohammad Heydari. Mohammad was a former soldier in Iran's Islamic Revolutionary Guard Corps. He was drawn into the military even though his father had died in the Iran-Iraq war. Mohammad served at a sensitive missile site in Tehran run by the IRGC. Mohammad was tired of living on a pittance of a salary like most IRGC members did, except those who were corrupt and had millions. He resented the fact that his father had died for the regime, and he was now married with children but could barely get by. Life in the IRGC was demanding for him. The IRGC expected Mohammad to work 80-hour weeks for the equivalent of $400. He and his family had no beds and slept on blankets on the floor.

He looked around at some of the top officers and saw them living in mansions, taking trips to villas in the lush hills of northern Tehran, and driving the fanciest of cars. Mohammad knew about it because he had access to classified information. He was to be a good soldier and sacrifice all for the Supreme Leader, but he wasn't supposed to ask too many questions. After all, he was promised the highest of the heavens in the next life. Mohammad was smarter than that. He felt like he had been betrayed, and the sacrifice of his father's life had been a sacrifice made for nothing he believed. Mohammad couldn't stand to see his son have so little. Over time, this made Mohammad bitter, and this is when he decided to take a trip to Turkey. On this trip, Mohammad would visit a building. On top of this building was a white and blue flag. The flag had two blue stripes, with the Star of David in the middle. The building was the Consulate of Israel.

Mohammad went into the building that housed the Israeli Consulate on the upper floors. He picked up the receiver of a phone and spoke into a camera to identify himself and his business at the consulate. He told them that he has information and wants to speak to a security officer. He's instructed to hold up his passport to the camera by the security guard working the entrance. After doing as instructed, he's told to wait. Twenty minutes later, two men in suits came to the lobby to escort Mohammad into the consulate.

In a room, Mohammad tells them how he feels cheated and lied to by the regime. He explains that he is living in near poverty while the officers skim millions of the nation's money to live a lifestyle of a king. They inquire about where he works and when he tells them that he was an analyst at Khatam Al-Anbiya – a well-known base run by the IRGC and home to sensitive missile technology– Mohammad gets the attention of the Mossad agents interviewing him.

"What do you want from us?" the Mossad agent asked in Farsi.

"Get me out of Iran. Help me and my family live in Europe or America. Help us have a life where I don't have to tell my son I can't buy him the nice things in the stores when we pass by."

The agent asks for Mohamed's contact information, leaves, and returns ten minutes later with a map. He shows Mohammad a satellite map of Khatam al-Anbiya military base and asked him to describe it. Mohammad stared at the image and after a few seconds, informs the man that the map he had shown him was not an image of Khatam Al Anbiya base. The agent smiles, he had been testing Mohammed. The agent then showed him a real satellite image of the military base. He pointed to different parts of the map and asked Mohammad to identify what they are. Mohammad does so easily. He then asked him to show exactly where he works, and Mohammad did so. The agent was interested because Mohammad pointed to an area where highly classified information on Iran's missile program was stored.

Mohammad worked in the office and had access to computer systems with the information on it. Mohammad also has detailed information on the IRGC's secret communication systems. Once the Mossad agent was satisfied, he asked Mohammad if he had told anyone about his whereabouts and that he was going to be going to the Israeli consulate that day. He replied no, even though he had confided in his wife. He was directed by the Mossad agent to gather information on IRGC Missile capabilities. He was to return to his work, retrieve documents, and send them to Mossad agents using an Israeli technology that sounded like a virtual machine that they placed on a USB. Initiation of the program started by clicking icons on a desktop in a specific pattern they were instructed to use by a Mossad agent. Once done, the screen would turn red, so Mohammed called the program Windows Red. After doing so, a program would open that would allow users to send encrypted messages and files directly to Mossad agents. With the program on the USB drive, this allowed users to send this information from their personal computers.

During his career as a spy, Mossad agents paid Mohammad in cash through Mossad accomplices inside Iran. The extra cash meant that he could do more things for his wife and children, but he was also growing increasingly concerned about getting caught. Spying for Israel meant certain execution, and IRGC Counter-Intelligence were experts at sniffing out spies.

Mohammad continued to ask his Mossad handlers for help to leave Iran but would be dismissed each time and told he needed to wait just a little while longer. Eventually, he's given what was supposed to be his last mission. After it was complete, he and his family would flee to Istanbul, and there they would be granted Israeli passports. With an Israel passport, anything was possible- Canada, Europe, America.

Plans were made for the assassination of an Iranian nuclear scientist named Masoud Ali Mohammadi. A bomb would be placed on a motorbike outside Masoud's home, and another Iranian trained by Mossad would detonate the bomb by remote. If the bomb failed to kill him, the other Iranian was to shoot him instead. Mohammad's last mission was to deliver a pistol, magazine, and bullets to the other Iranian working for Mossad. That Iranian was Majid Jamali Fashi. Majid was a kickboxer that often traveled to compete and sought asylum in several foreign countries. He thought Israel would be a helpful conduit in achieving his goal.

Mohammad met with Majid in a secret Tehran location. After using coded language to confirm his identity, Mohammad handed over the weapon. At the time, Mohammad had no idea who Majid was or the mission he was carrying out. It wouldn't be until after Majid's arrest and publicized confession on Iranian television that Mohammad had a name and a face to the man he had given the gun to. On the morning of January 12, 2010, the mission had been successful, and Iranian Masoud Ali Mohammadi was killed in an explosion outside his home.

Iranian intelligence agents arrested Majid after the assassination with the pistol Mohammad had given him still in his possession. While Mohammad didn't know Majid, Majid knew some details about Mohammad, and in his subsequent confession Iranian agents were able to eventually track down Mohammed, and arrest him. Pressure was brought down on Mohammad's wife. The case against him was solidified when she confirmed the accusations made by the MOIS. He had told her about his Mossad connection.

Mohammad approached me to tell me he was in Ward 209 a few cell doors down from me, and could hear me constantly arguing with the guards. The first thing I remember when meeting him was the sadness in his eyes. Mohammad would ask me for cigarettes even though I told him several times that I didn't smoke. He was the first person that I had been able to talk to in eighteen months that didn't threaten or torment me. As he told this story to me, he maintained that he was facing some prison time, and then he would be free. He downplayed the situation to me and everyone else in Ward 350. I couldn't help but notice his chain-smoking and the long tear-filled prayers he would make. The sadness in his eyes, the smoking, and the prayers of desperation would make sense to all of us soon.

One evening, Mohammad's name was called over the loudspeaker to get ready to see the doctor. The day before, he had a visit with his family and mentioned that he was feeling sick and needed medication. When he didn't return, we thought that his health might have been worse than we knew, and they had taken him to a hospital. It wasn't until after roll call the next morning when we turned on the news and saw the headline.

"Mohammed Heydari executed by hanging for cooperating with Israel."

We were in shock. The man that I had been talking to each day and every night, who had just been living and breathing was now hanging at the end of a rope. Iranian media displayed photographs of Mohammad hanging from a rope in a room with Judge Salavati, the same judge who sentenced me to death, standing in front of him. Ward 350 was silent that day. Those that were on death row were especially quiet. Even though the death sentence hung over their heads, seeing a fellow inmate executed made it even more real to them.

After the shock of Mohammad's death had faded, people began to talk about his execution. Many didn't believe that Majid Jamali Fashi named Mohammad after he was arrested. Rumors began to spread that either the Israelis or the Turkish government made a deal with Iranian officials and agreed to sell the identities of those

Iranians working for them in exchange for a prisoner swap or other political concessions. Another rumor was that vendors and restaurant owners in the area surrounding the embassies in Istanbul were taking photos of Iranian-looking males entering the buildings and sending the photos to Iranian intelligence. Iranian intelligence would then cross-reference the photos with Iranian entry and exit stamps on passports. Both rumors gained traction because both scenarios were plausible. Then again, in prison, and even more so in an Iranian prison gossiping, and spreading rumours was a favorite pastime. Mohammad's death prompted prisoners to wonder how they were caught or accused.

Mohammad's bunk became a highly sought-after piece of real estate and was quickly doled out to one of the more senior prisoners. Some avoided the bunk considering it "bad luck" that an executed man had once slept there. His belongings were packed up into a trash bag that would be picked up by his family. Seeing that bag and a man's existence reduced to what could fit inside a trash bag had a profound impact on us all. Whoever he was or did he had a family, a wife and child. I thought about how that would feel for his wife, or mother to come pick up a trash bag with his prison belongings. This reminded me of when as a US Marine returning from combat and seeing the parents of Marines we lost being consoled, and handed folded American flags as they sobbed. I couldn't help but feel bad for his family. While in the case of the Marines their loved ones were honored with folded American flags, Mohammed's family would find a stiff dead body in the morgue with his neck blackened, and wrangled from the hanging, and a garbage bag with his belongings.

In prison, everything is always changing, and with Mohammad's bunk filled by another inmate and his belongings removed, Mohammad was forgotten. The whole ordeal revealed the heartlessness of prison. He would only remain in the painful memories of his mother. She was seen sobbing earlier that day by inmates who had gone to court. She just found out that her son's sentence had been carried out. She would need to identify his body and then sign for it so she could retrieve him from the prison morgue.

☒

Chapter Nineteen:
The Electrician

Asghar Padashi is another man I met in Ward 350. Asghar had been a member of the IRGC and had fought in the Iran-Iraq war at a very early age. Inmates were just intrigued by me, they had so many questions about America, and so many of them believed that I was some elite CIA operative, and wanted to talk about spycraft. Many of them also wanted advice on how they were caught by MOIS, and if I thought the CIA may have betrayed them. He was different in a sense that he revealed to me his motivations for working for Mossad wasn't based on a particular bias, but because he enjoyed the thrill of operations. He had been sentenced to death which eventually was reduced to a 10-year sentence for his cooperation having given MOIS details on Mossad tactics. He suffered an injury in military training, and left the IRGC after the war. He struggled to find employment and decided that with his background in electrical engineering, he would open an electrical shop where he would help residents and businesses with various electrical repairs. Asghar received a phone call from a Turkish man inviting him to Istanbul to discuss doing business with his firm. While confused by the call or how the Turk even knew about him, he agreed to make the trip in hopes that he could secure additional business there. They met in a Turkish bazaar where they made small talk over coffee at a café. Asghar was at first given real electrical work, but after a few meetings the conversation turned into a proposition to work for Mossad.

Asghar's background in engineering, and having been a member of the IRGC made him an attractive agent. He was told that Mossad would invest in him. I recalled Asghar's eyes lighting up whenever he would discuss his work for Mossad. When he discussed his motivation, he said that he was someone who liked to conduct operations and mostly agreed to work for Mossad for the thrill of the work. Taken aback by this statement, considering the risks involved, he seemed genuine. Asghar was first given training at a military base in Israel. Already having a company registered in Iran provided the perfect cover for his overseas travel. His first trip would be to Bangkok, Thailand, a hotbed for global spy activity due to the high level of tourists visiting the country each year. Many Iranian inmates arrested for cooperation with Mossad also traveled to Bangkok, where Iranians and Israelis could enter Visa-Free.

Asghar was to meet with handlers there who would interview him, and subject him to a polygraph. He met two Israeli men, both of whom spoke fluent Farsi, in a prearranged hotel room. After passing the polygraph, Asghar received a laptop to take back with him and departed Bangkok two days after arriving to return to Tehran. Asghar was given very basic tasks at first communicating with his handlers with the same computer program Mohammad had used, but Asghar's handlers wanted visual access to him, so the laptop given to him was enabled with remote camera access. Asghar would open the laptop, and click on the icons in a specific sequence as a code to gain access to the program. Once in, he used a program that enabled him to send and receive messages using Steganography.

Steganography embedded messages in images that could be decoded and was the practice of hiding a file or message within another file. The benefit of using steganography over encryption was that encrypted packets coming and leaving the Iranian internet would raise suspicion. Even if the Iranians couldn't decrypt the message, they could track encrypted messages being sent back and forth, creating a digital footprint to hunt someone down and track their activities. Steganography traveled under the cover of a normal file or picture being sent.

The idea of using the laptop and this program was to make the communication look as natural as possible, while also giving Asghar some protection should his laptop be seized at an Iranian port of entry.

Anyone fishing into his laptop would have to know the sequence of icons to click to open the communications portal. The program would not leave data on the system, and if it did, they would be pictures that would require a proprietary Mossad decryption software to decode the pictures into their original hidden message.

Regular check-in protocols were implemented so that if Asghar didn't check in with his laptop for a certain period of time, his Mossad handlers would be alerted that he had possibly been arrested. To begin, Mossad would give him bogus missions designed to test his ability and feel him out. They would task him with taking pictures of random businesses or sites that had no intelligence value.

These bogus missions also served to get Asghar comfortable with conducting spycraft. As time went on and they gained confidence in him, Asghar was invited to Israel for more in-depth training. He didn't know it at the time, but Asghar was being groomed to join the Mossad nuclear scientists assassination teams Israel was building inside the country.

Asghar couldn't travel to Israel on an Iranian passport, so they used an outdated spy technique that involved passport swapping. Asghar would depart Tehran for Istanbul, Turkey, on his Iranian passport, and an Israeli Mossad agent would simultaneously travel from Israel into Turkey or some other country with accommodating travel conditions for Israelis. Once both of them were in the country, the Israeli would swap the picture on his Israeli passport with that of Asghar. Asghar would surrender his Iranian passport to the Israeli who would then wait in Turkey until Asghar had returned. Now Asghar would fly into Israel with the Israeli passport given to him and meet his handlers at a secret training facility in Israel. When he arrived at the training center, he was introduced to another Iranian, Ali Reza. The two would know each other by codenames and were instructed not to give identifying information to one another for their protection in case of capture.

Ali Reza was also a former IRGC member that had been recruited by Mossad, and Ali Reza and Asghar would act as a team. Ali Reza would be the driver, and Asghar would be the technician for upcoming missions. Their training in Israel consisted of evasive driving, surveillance, firearms, communication devices, electronic tools used for technical eavesdropping, and tactical explosives used to kill Iranian nuclear scientists. After the training, Ali Reza and Asghar would go separate ways and meet in Iran only when specific missions called for it. Asghar would fly back to Istanbul, get his Iranian passport, and then fly back to Tehran.

His next task was to fly to Bangkok and obtain a sophisticated, classified, and technical eavesdropping tool that would enable Israeli spy satellites to intercept phone calls of nuclear scientists it was targeting. The sensitive device was hidden inside a vehicle battery charger. The device cover was chosen to match Asghar's background as an electrician in case he was questioned upon returning to Tehran. Once past security and in Iran, Asghar received instructions on removing the eavesdropping device, and how to prepare it for placement near the address of the home where the Iranian nuclear scientist was living. Asghar met with Ali Reza, who drove him to the location where he was to place the device.

Asghar was instructed to create a cover for the device that looked like an electric fuse box that matched the many fuse box doors found on commercial buildings in Tehran. Asghar arrived at the location and exited the vehicle while Ali Reza waited in the car and acted as the lookout.

Asghar was to drill the fake fusebox compartment that contained the electronic surveillance device into the side of a commercial building picked out by Mossad. With the device in place, Asghar would leave the area and leave the device there for several days while Israeli satellites used the device to intercept communications of persons of interest in the area. Asghar and Ali Reza were a team that would move around different areas of Tehran, installing and removing these electronic devices enabling Mossad to collect vital signals intelligence on Iranian targets.

With Ali Reza and Asghar completing missions successfully, Mossad agents felt they were ready for something more advanced. Mossad had intel on the movements of a nuclear scientist and tasked the pair with planting an explosive device in a tree near the entrance of the scientist's house. Ali Reza and Asghar would remotely detonate the explosive once the scientist left his home. While Asghar had no wife or children, Ali Reza was married to a woman who had a brother currently serving in the IRGC. For reasons that were never clear to me, the wife knew about Ali Reza's relationship with Mossad. During an argument with Ali Reza, she told her brother in the IRGC about her husband's affiliation leading to Ali Reza's arrest.

When Ali Reza didn't respond to messages for several days, Asghar was spooked and fled the country to Turkey. With the mission in jeopardy and Ali Reza in IRGC custody, Asghar was in contact with his Mossad contacts and was making plans to flee Turkey to Israel. Asghar, however, had doubts about his Mossad handlers, and for whatever reason, believed he would be killed if he went to Israel. He decided to turn himself in and called contacts in Iran who put him in touch with IRGC agents who assured him if he turned himself in, he would be spared the death penalty. Ali Reza had already given him up and confessed to the murder plot of the Iranian scientist. Asghar turned himself in and was given a life sentence, which eventually was reduced further to 10 years.

Chapter Twenty:
Digital Walk-Ins

I kept to myself in Ward 350 and frequented the yard. Inside, I felt like I couldn't get enough air. Evin was elevated and surrounded by mountains. The air was thinner, but at times the breeze would come down the mountainside and into the prison yard. I would look up, close my eyes, breathe in, and be. The fresh air helped me feel alive. One day while I was outside in the yard, I was approached by two inmates. They bonded with me over a cigarette one had in his hand. As I inhaled, they began to explain to me how they had been recruited by the CIA and wanted to know if I had any idea how they got caught.

They told me that intelligence agents in the MOIS had pictures of them meeting with CIA agents in hotels in Dubai, Malaysia, Armenia, and even Georgia. MOIS even knew the names that CIA agents gave them. A CIA agent named Mark – a fake name, I'm sure – was the handler for many of the inmates in Ward 350 who didn't know each other until they all ended up in Evin together. The inmates said they denied all the charges levied against them by MOIS in their interrogations until MOIS Iranian intelligence agents told them the names of their CIA handlers, the names of the hotels they met at, and the email addresses they used to communicate. When MOIS interrogators told them of intimate details they all caved, and signed their confessions sparing themselves a prolonged period in solitary confinement.

One of the inmates was a contractor for Iran's nuclear program. GR had a great disdain for the regime and for Islam itself. He had grown immensely fed up with life in Iran and loved everything that was American. GR was smart and intense. He had a background in engineering and worked for an engineering contract firm. He desperately wanted to move abroad with his family but lacked the money and legal avenue to do so. He either needed to get a student visa or immigrate somehow. Doing so to the US or Canada would be no easy task. After much consideration, he decided that to make money and fast track immigration to the US, he would cooperate with the CIA.

He told me that he simply went to the CIA website and clicked on the 'submit a tip' section. This was common amongst many of the Iranian inmates who had cooperated with the CIA. Very few of them had been actively recruited by the CIA and were essentially digital walk-ins. On the submission page, GR eluded to the type of data he had and gave a non-attributable Gmail address. Days later, he received an email instructing him to call a number or to respond to the email by answering several questions. The questions asked why he wanted to work with the CIA, the type of information he had, the type of information he had access to, how long he had access to this data, and if contacted again, where he would be able to meet with CIA agents.

After the exchange of several emails, the CIA was interested and arranged to meet him in Dubai, but GR wanted confirmation that he was indeed talking to the CIA and was told that he could contact any

US Embassy, ask to speak to the security officer on duty, and give them a code given to him in the email. The security officer at the US Embassy would read him back a second code only the sender of the email would have been able to transmit to him. GR called the US Embassy in Azerbaijan, and they confirmed his email contacts. GR paid for the trip to Dubai from his own account, and when he arrived at the hotel in Dubai was paid back in US dollars, plus a little extra for his cooperation. The relationship would continue with GR gaining access to engineering documents on the Natanz nuclear site he had been contracting in. At one point, GR had been given a handheld scanner to scan engineering blueprints and other sensitive documents and deliver them to the CIA.

Throughout the relationship, GR would deliver hundreds of documents reports to CIA handlers. He delivered these reports in person, sometimes at various sites around Iran, but primarily in Dubai, Cyprus, and Kuala Lumpur. Four years into their relationship, GR wanted to call it quits and asked that the CIA help relocate him and his family to the United States. And then, out of nowhere, GR was arrested and taken into interrogation. After MOIS revealed all the information they had gathered, GR admitted to cooperating with the CIA. After my release, I had seen reports in the media about a 'communications method using internet sites' that had been used by the CIA to message spies in Iran. It had been compromised and brought about many arrests. Iran shared this information with China, and there were arrests in China, too. After this news broke, it was reported that the CIA Head of the Iran Desk was fired.

One of the prisoners that had been convicted for spying had met with his handler once he was released. The former prisoner wanted to know his take on why Iranian interrogators had so much detailed information about his relationship with the CIA. The handler told him that the CIA was working on it and that they could do better, and even gave him $30k in cash to make amends for the years of imprisonment he endured. I was amazed at how little effort the CIA had to exert to attract people to work for them simply based on their affinity for the USA, or in hopes of making it to America one day.

It appeared to me that a mosquito couldn't move in Iran without Mossad or the CIA knowing about it by the amount of prisoners inside Ward 350 who had been convicted of working for them. If this was only the ones caught, how many more were there who hadn't? At the same time, the MOIS had filled its prisons with those same cooperators. We would see a new prisoner walk in from interrogations and solitary confinement almost daily. They all had the same look of pain in their eyes, all wore the same full beards, and all had the same stench after being caught spying for a foreign nation. This happened so often that upon meeting a new entrant for the first time, after only a few sentences, or just revealing their occupation the more senior inmates would know what they were convicted of. "CIA?" we'd tell the new arrival. "Yeah, how did you know?" was the usual startled response.

For most, their motivations were to escape Iran and reside in Western countries. The handlers dangled that possibility in front of them but required them to prove themselves first by providing valuable information. In rare cases, the CIA directly sought out and recruited Iranians under false pretenses before eventually revealing who they were. One instance was a prisoner with initials, MR. MR had a degree in telecommunications and had several years of experience working for China's Huawei Technologies in Iran. He had firsthand knowledge of technologies Huawei had supplied Iranian Intelligence to be able to monitor, spy on, and track wireless users throughout Iran. The US reports on concerns about Huawei having military ties and being a pseudo part of China's security apparatus were true, according to MR, who said he had worked directly on those projects.

MR told me he had received an email from a company based in Dubai looking to hire a telecom consultant for contract work. The pay rate was attractive and covered travel expenses to Dubai, a place MR had already been interested in visiting one day. MR gladly accepted and met with members of the consultancy group in Dubai to advise on opportunities in Iranian telecom. After a few visits, MR began to suspect that this was not a random consultancy as more questions were being asked concerning Huawei's involvement in providing spying tools for the wireless carrier RighTel. His suspicions were confirmed when MR was invited to the US for a consulting project where, in a Las Vegas hotel, individuals revealed that they were CIA. While MR was never clear about how Iranian intelligence knew about his work with the CIA, he believes his travel patterns, and his internet searches about obtaining residency in the USA led to his arrest.

The CIA recruited other prisoners in Evin after they had applied to US universities. In their admission applications, they would note their place of work. This was of particular interest if their place of work was a sensitive Iranian military facility or if they had studied or conducted research in nuclear, missile, or, or sensitive communications technology. The prisoners in Evin were a portrait of the status of international relationships at that time. America was interested in preventing Iran's nuclear program, the transfer of sensitive weapons and technology, and preventing attacks against Americans. Israel was interested in taking out Iranian nuclear scientists and targeting important Iranian officials. Both used Iranians desperate for a better life to achieve their goals and abandoned them when they were caught. None of these cases indicated an effort on behalf of the US to induce regime change, or based on a hatred for Islam despite this being the common narrative put forth by Iranian officials.

Chapter Twenty-One:
The Games Played by the Ministry of Intelligence

The population of Ward 350 was made up of career spies, university professors, academics, assassins, bloggers, activists, and the occasional foreigner. Ward 8 of Evin Prison had an entire wing designated for foreigners. Many of these inmates were Nigerian drug dealers who had come to Iran to purchase crystal meth. Iran had become a major exporter of crystal meth with hidden meth labs all over Tehran. Iranian law was extremely harsh on meth dealers with as little as 3 grams warranting an immediate death penalty.

In Ward 350, we had one Korean convicted of spying, a Slovakian, and the sole American, me. The Slovakian was arrested for supporting pornographic websites inside Iran on servers in Slovakia. Economic woes in Iran had caused an explosion in temporary marriages, prostitution, and drug use. He was sentenced to life imprisonment until the Slovakian government was able to have him released in diplomatic negotiations.

Ward 350 was dubbed Evin University due to the high level of education amongst the prisoners. Inmates would organize poetry night, book club, group prayer, exercise, and cultural nights. I was amazed to see groups of political oppositionists who would be praised in Western society being treated like terrorists in Iran's judicial system and serving extremely harsh sentences. One university professor who had been arrested for speaking out against corruption had been organizing rallies inside the prison in protest. This activity made him a target of the MOIS. He was transferred from Ward 350 to another prison on the outskirts of Tehran in a ward filled with violent criminals and drug dealers. What was certain cooperation between the violent prisoners and MOI resulted in the professor being attacked with razors on both sides of his face.

Prisoners who saw him in the hospital said he looked like the Joker. Whenever any prisoner would protest or videos or text of a political nature to news outlets like BBC, they would be dealt with in this manner. Intimidation, and even exile to a far off Iranian province were suppressive tools used by MOIS against political opponents.

The Iranian regime believed that anything was allowed if Islam or the regime were threatened. For many in power, the regime and Islam were the same, so dissidents speaking out against the regime were also speaking out against Islam. Those against Islam were at war with God. Those who were at war with God were worthy of the harshest punishments. You could be a serial murderer, and in the eyes of the regime, you were simply a criminal who was worthy of repentance and a pardon. A thief, drug dealer, or rapist all had the option to be released. Insult the Supreme Leader of Iran? That was unforgivable, and in the eyes of the regime, you were worse than a serial rapist.

The resolve of those men prepared to deal with the harshest consequences for their political beliefs was inspiring to me. They were often offered shortened sentences or release if they made public statements that they were wrong for their actions and asked for forgiveness.

They refused. While I was extremely impressed with these men and considered the Iranian regime brutal in its treatment of political opposition, I didn't see in this group a viable replacement for the Iranian regime. I saw in them opposing factions, daily arguments, and a lack of a coherent, unified message.

Throughout my time in Ward 350, I would come to know many, but there was a separation between those arrested on security crimes and those arrested for political cases. I was somewhere in between as I was initially charged with spying, but the reason for my arrest was political. Later, when I would be sentenced for cooperating with a hostile country for my military service, the lines as to where I fell within these two groups blurred even more. The political detainees considered it an insult by the regime to house them with spies. It was another effort to discredit their dissenting opinions. Many of these political detainees were falsely accused of having ties to foreign intelligence services as a means to discredit them and housing them with legitimate spies fed into the MOIS' narrative.

A man in Ward 350 told me the story of how he signed his "confession" in the interrogation room of Ward 209. He had gone months in solitary. He refused to accept any confession that would allow MOIS agents to sentence him. He had done nothing wrong. He protested and exposed financial corruption. The MOIS accused him of trying to overthrow the government. Overthrowing the government was a blanket charge MOIS applied to anyone that disagreed with the regime in an organized manner. If you and a few friends protested, they could hit you with 'attempting to overthrow the government' charge. However, this charge carried a longer prison sentence than simple protesting. Arresting political dissidents on charges of overthrowing the government was a tactic MOIS used to silence them and keep them in prison longer.

The man continued to refuse to accept that charge and endured all the pressures and mistreatment that came with being placed in Ward 209. One day he was brought into the interrogation room and told to remove his blindfold. He found his wife sitting in the interrogation room sobbing. MOIS had arrested her, and she was now sitting in her own solitary confinement cell. MOI agents quickly removed him from the room and used his love for his wife against him. They told him he had to confess to attempting to overthrow the government and save your wife; otherwise, she would be charged, too. He immediately confessed and signed every document put in front of him by MOIS agents. His fate was sealed.

Chapter Twenty-Two:
The Ambassador's Son

In February of 2012, the Obama administration sanctioned the Iranian Central Bank. The sanctions delivered a crippling economic blow to the regime making the transfer of funds abroad, even for the most basic reasons, difficult and, in some cases, impossible. It made it so difficult that Iranian Embassies and consulates all around the world were unable to receive cash from the homeland to fund diplomatic operations. Salaries for personnel and other vital expenses were no longer fundable by bank transfer. The regime was in an impossible situation, and their solution was to fund embassies by ferrying Embassy employees to and from Iran carrying suitcases full of cash.

An inmate in Ward 350, HR, practiced his English with me from time-to-time during walks in the prison yard. He had lived in Toronto, Canada for a year, and being from Michigan; I visited Toronto many times. We had plenty to talk about. After a few conversations, he began to share with me his background and mentioned that he had lived in Paris for years before moving to Canada and that he had maintained Iranian and French citizenship. He spoke very good French and began to reminisce about the many things he loved about France. I asked him how he had lived in two of the best cities in the world, Paris and Toronto, and ended up in Evin. He confided in me that his father had worked for the Iranian Foreign Ministry in France. He enjoyed his life in Paris but knew that eventually, his family would get sent back to Iran. He had become accustomed to his European lifestyle and dreaded the thought of leaving it behind.

Once the Iranian Central Bank was sanctioned, on his father's recommendation, he was tasked with traveling between Paris and Tehran and delivering cash the embassy needed to function. When HR would visit Tehran, he grew depressed. He could see the impact that economic sanctions and a hardline regime were having on the country. He became more convinced that he needed to do something to avoid having to come back to Iran and being forced to live there for the rest of his life. HR carried a few hundred thousand dollars with him on each trip and avoided questions from French airport personnel due to his diplomatic status. He knew he would need to act soon and decided to put his plan into action.

On one particular trip, he was given the equivalent of $730,000 US dollars in Euros. Once he landed in Paris, rather than deliver the money to the Embassy, he went missing. HR checked into a Paris hotel and paid cash for his stay. He then began to use a series of currency exchanges and money transfer networks to move the money from Paris to Toronto. It took him almost a month to move the money. He received frantic calls, texts, and emails from his family, which he ignored. HR took a train from Paris to Madrid, Spain. He chose Madrid because he was afraid that the Iranian Embassy had placed a block on his travel in France. He thought that by flying out from another country, he would avoid detection in France.

With his French passport in hand, HR's one-way flight landed in Canada, where he could enter visa-free and stay for up to 90 days. HR planned to eventually seek asylum in the country under the auspices that he was a political opponent to the Iranian regime. Having put off frantic phone calls from his father and other family members in Iran for too long now, HR felt it was safe now that he was on Canadian soil to finally break the news. Scared of his father's reaction, he told his mother that for years now, he had seen his role in the Iranian Foreign

Ministry as a "dead-end" career and a life that would eventually return him to Iran where he no longer wanted a future. The promotion system in Iran was fraught with cronyism, and he would never achieve the level of a career that he aspired to. He didn't share the same ideology of the regime, wanted to see a democratic Iran, and didn't understand the regime's obsession with "dominating" the Middle East.

He wanted to see an Iran that focused on tapping the vast potential of its people, leaving each Iranian to his own way of political thought and independent thinking. HR and many Iranian youths recall troubled childhoods growing up with regular propaganda that they should hate other nations and wish death upon them. He didn't want that for his children whenever he decided to get married. While his mother was most likely more tolerant than his father, his father delivered serious warnings to him through his mother. His father said his standing at the embassy would be ruined, and the Iranian Ministry of Intelligence had already recalled him back to Tehran.

Weeks of calls with his family and complaints from his father about the implications began to take a toll on him. His father would soon be charged with aiding and abetting the son. He was facing jail time, as well as being on the hook for the $730k. HR's mother and father's home could be seized and sold unless the son returned the funds, and surrendered himself to MOIS While HR was desperate to avoid prison and the thought of returning to Iran shamed, and facing prison time was worse than death for him, he couldn't let his father, and mother be destroyed for what he did. Only a few months after HR executed his botched escape plan, he was on a flight back to Tehran. He would have to look at the Toronto skyline for the last time aboard a flight back to Tehran.

HR was detained at Imam Khomeini International Airport and rushed by guards to Ward 209 detention center. MOIS agents tried to get him to confess that he was a spy and influenced him to run off with the money. After weeks of interrogation and solitary, they settled for the embezzlement charge. HR was sentenced to 2 years of prison and given a fine that was one and a half times the amount he stole. His father attended the court proceeding and began to punch and slap him in front of the judge once the sentence was announced and told him he was no longer his son in front of the courtroom. He admitted that was the absolute low point in his life. Now he was walking the yard with an Iranian-American in Evin prison telling his story about the time that he almost got away with ¾ of a million dollars to start a brand new life in the posh metropolitan city of Toronto.

Several other inmates had also been in Evin on sanctions-related issues. US Sanctions on Iran created a global network of sanction evaders that used front companies and intermediaries to deliver to Iran just about anything it wanted. Under sanctions, most items could still be acquired, but usually at four times the price. Russian, Chinese, and Turkish companies played a massive role in this global network. A Chinese company could buy sensitive technologies, machinery, and equipment from the US. The Chinese company would turn around and sell it to a company in Kazakhstan. The company in Kazakhstan who would deliver it to the real end buyer in Iran. Russians set up companies in Hong Kong specifically for this purpose. In case the plot was discovered by US authorities, at worst case, the US company would no longer do business with that entity, but the Russian or Chinese would rarely face any fines, or prosecution as they would keep themselves, and all their assets outside of the US financial, and judicial system. However, US Intelligence would often realize who the end buyer was and begin to add names to its global watchlists. Occasionally, those individuals would make a mistake and take a trip to a country where US extradition requests would be processed. Countries like Thailand, Spain, France, the UK, and Malaysia are all countries where sanctions violators have gone and been intercepted by US authorities.

Chapter Twenty-Three
The Inner Circle

It was normal in Ward 350 to be cordial with everyone but have few close friends. The people I was closest to were Mokhtar, Eman, and Shojaei. Mokhtar was a Kurdish-Iranian professional bodybuilder. He was 6'5" and 240 lbs. of muscle. At the time of my arrest, I was 5'10" and 220 lbs. but my time in solitary confinement saw my weight fall all the way down to 165 lbs. Mokhtar and I were inseparable in the gym. We worked out hard every day with what little weights we had. We made barbells from empty plastic jugs we filled with water and used string to make handles to curl with. We spent about two hours every day in the exercise area working out. Exercise kept me sane, and I was regaining the muscular physique I had before my arrest helped me regain my identity.

Mokhtar was serving ten years for his unwitting involvement in running surveillance on an Iranian nuclear scientist. The Israelis recruited him during a trip visiting his family in Kurdistan, Iraq. He told me that the Israelis never identified themselves as being Israeli and used a Kurdish intermediary to convince Mokhtar that the individual was a random person who owed a monetary debt. Mokhtar was to follow him and gather information for the Kurdish intermediary so the man could find out details about him to help police enforce the debt. MOIS agents providing counter-surveillance on the nuclear scientist spotted Mokhtar and made the arrest. Despite his pleas that he had no idea, he was sentenced to 10 years.

To my knowledge, he is still serving that sentence at the time of this writing. Mokhtar was a really great guy. Despite his bad luck, he had one of the most positive attitudes of anyone at Evin. His energy and motivation were contagious, and he helped motivate me to do my time and not let me time do me.

My second close friend was Eman. Eman was an incredibly smart and talented hacker. A computer programming prodigy, Eman was a master at software engineering and was recruited by the IRGC at a young age to assist them in offensive hacking operations. He had been heavily involved in the cyber-attack on Saudi Aramco that infected over 30,000 computers and cost millions in damage. IRGC used one of its many front companies to hire Eman as a consultant.

Everyone at the company knew that they were working for IRGC, but since these were not military personnel, they were paid by front companies. The difference between this civilian group of hackers and IRGC personnel involved in cybersecurity operations was that they had freedoms the IRGC personnel did not. They didn't have to live on a military base, could go on vacation whenever they wanted and were freelancers. Eman was involved in the vulnerability scanning of various targets around the globe. Using unknown methods, the US government tracked Eman. During a vacation to Armenia, Eman and his Iranian girlfriend were approached by a man at the hotel where they were staying. The man, visibly American or European, made small talk and set Eman up to disclose his profession as a computer programmer. The man said he wanted to keep in touch with Eman about possible opportunities, and they exchanged information.

Over the next few weeks, the man would maintain contact with Eman and eventually invited him to Kuala Lumpur, Malaysia, for a business meeting about technology-related projects he wanted to pursue in the Middle East and offer Eman freelance work. Once Eman arrived at the hotel, 3 CIA officers confronted him. They put in front of him a file they had on him with overwhelming evidence that he was involved in Iranian cyber-attacks and was considered a cyber-terrorist under American and International Law. The lead CIA officer threatened Eman that they were prepared to enforce a warrant and extradition request on him at this very moment unless he cooperated and divulged everything he knew to prevent further attacks. Eman immediately caved and pleaded not to be arrested. It was probably an empty threat. He explained that there were no good programming jobs in Iran, and he was using his IRGC salary to support himself temporarily until he could afford to move abroad. He explained that he had no issues with America, and he hoped to move there someday and work in tech.

The agents used those statements to offer Eman a deal. They would temporarily suspend the warrant out for Eman if he agreed to help them prevent further cyberattacks by cooperating with them. He was to go back to his place of employment and report back to CIA officers using an agreed-upon Gmail account. Eman would cooperate with the CIA for 18 months. He provided information on IRGC cyber capabilities as well as the identities of other IRGC hackers involved. He earned thousands of dollars for these efforts. Payment would regularly come from CIA by postal mail from Malaysia. Fresh US Dollar bills would be placed inside of a book that had the middle pages cutout. Eman was able to buy a small apartment near Tehran and planned on proposing to his girlfriend. Then he was arrested. He confessed to his CIA relationship and was given a lengthy prison sentence. After my release, I learned that Iranian intelligence had hacked the computer of the manager of my freedom campaign in hopes of obtaining information. I wonder if it was someone that Eman knew from his days doing similar work.

The other person I trusted was Shojaei. Shojaei was a male flight attendant on now blacklisted Mahan Air, an Iranian regional airliner known for flights to nearby destinations in Iraq, Turkey, Afghanistan, North Africa, and Southeast Asia. The Iranian Revolutionary guards partly own Mahan Air. Shojaei was on flights to Libya when the Iranian government used Mahan Air as a cover to ferry injured fighters to hospitals in Tehran. These were fighters involved in the overthrow of the Gaddafi regime. Iran blamed Muammar al-Gaddafi for the disappearance of one of its revered clerics. Imam Musa Al-Sadr. Sadr disappeared on a visit to Libya in 1978, and it is widely believed that Gaddafi had him killed to prevent the proselytizing of the Shia Islamic faith in other Arab countries as Sadr had so successfully done in Southern Lebanon. This proselytizing eventually led to the militant group, Hezbollah.

Sadr was in Libya to seek Gaddafi's help to mediate conflicts the Shi'ites of southern Lebanon were having with Palestinian factions using the South of Lebanon to stage attacks on Israel, leaving the Shi'ites of southern Lebanon open to Israeli retaliation. Sadr was never seen after that meeting, and it remains a mystery today. Shojaei was part of an effort to work with Libyan rebels to discover his fate. On other trips from Tehran to Damascus, Shojaei witnessed strange cargo being loaded that he believed to be weapons caches heading to Syria to support beleaguered Syrian leader Bashar Al-Assad violent suppression of popular protests in his country. The occupants of many of these flights were IRGC military personnel and not ordinary travelers.

During a layover in Istanbul, Turkey, Shojaei offered his information to the Israeli consulate there. His motives were money, and the opportunity to relocate out of Iran into Europe for which his Mossad handlers agreed to facilitate if he provided information of value. Shojaei was tasked with reporting on the flights, obtaining photos of passengers, and flight manifests if possible. Shojaei was never clear about how he was caught, but his hunch was that Turkish counter-intelligence running surveillance on the Israeli consulate had outed him under a secretive intelligence cooperation agreement Turkey had with Iran. Shojaei hadn't gotten very far in his relationship with Mossad and was sentenced to 5 years in Evin for approaching the Israeli consulate. Most Iranians caught on espionage charges in Iran tended to have a hatred for the regime and desperation to leave Iran. One of the more unspoken impacts of US Sanctions on Iran and the economic difficulty it created for ordinary Iranian citizens is the increase in Iranians willing to sell information to the West in exchange for help escaping Iran and its hardships.

These individuals were not ideologues, and they were not willing to share this information to score one for the other guy, they simply wanted to have a normal life.

Chapter Twenty-Four:
Life on the Outside and the World Inside

The last member of my inner circle was Majid. Majid was the cellphone guy. During monthly conjugal visits with his wife, she would strategically hide a cellphone in her undergarments. Female guards wouldn't search those areas thoroughly for cultural reasons. Majid was a political oppositionist and would bring in the phones for high-level political detainees. Ward 350 would frequently put out statements to BBC Farsi and other networks covering Iran. Political detainees would send pictures of poor prison conditions to human rights organizations. These poor prison conditions included gigantic rats that we would have to frequently kill with broomsticks, a massive infestation of bed bugs that would sting and drink your blood at night, open sewers running in the yard causing sickness and filling the prison with an awful stench, and lack of warm water. People were being denied phone calls, blocked from seeing their lawyers, were not receiving necessary medical care, and were beaten by guards when they were angry.

Not all the guards took enjoyment from causing us pain. The smuggling depended on a guard who was a sympathizer to some of the political detainees. The guard was eventually arrested. The leaked statements bothered the MOIS so much that they installed signal jammers and electronic eavesdropping tools on the rooftop of Ward 350. At times, the signal was jammed, and at times open.

When open, any signals leaving Ward 350 were likely under surveillance.

Despite the electronic countermeasures, pictures and voice messages were still getting out. The media playing back videos and statements from inside the prison was an extreme embarrassment to the MOIS because it made them look incompetent.

After roll call one morning, everyone was told on the loudspeaker to stay in their cells.

Seconds later, at least 50 guards with batons came marching into the prison. Everyone was ordered to remain in their cells while the guards thrashed and tore everything apart. They knifed pillows and blankets and searched in the lining of prisoners' underwear for SIM cards and used electronic tools to find cellphones. They recovered 23 cellphones and other electronic devices. A photo of all the phones laid out on the table was broadcasted on Iranian state news that night.

They publicly gave themselves a pat on the back. Several cellphones were hiding in a cut out can of shaving cream. These phones were not found. At the same time that MOIS was patting themselves on the back on Iranian state television, details of the raid were published to BBC Farsi and other networks.

During that raid, many of the political prisoners were struck with batons and sent to solitary confinement. Members of the political opposition discovered one of the inmates had snitched on them and told officials about the phones. They confronted him. After all, several of their friends had been badly beaten, sent to solitary, and had additional prison time added to their sentence. MOIS would often recruit prisoners to act as snitches in return for additional conjugal visits or furloughs away from the prison. The political detainees confronted the snitch in the cooking room. They started by breaking raw eggs on his face before they started lobbing kicks and punches on him. Once he endured the full beating, they lifted him headfirst into the trashcan and then threw more eggs on him. We couldn't help but laugh, seeing him come out of the trash, bruised, and covered with raw egg yolk. The beating he endured was mild and demonstrated the civility of the political detainees. The snitch continued to carry out his sentence in Ward 350 without further incident.

Fights in other prison wards containing drug offenders and violent criminals involved stabbings and beatings, resulting in permanent damage or death. The most violent incident I witnessed was when I was getting treated for a stomach infection in the infirmary. I was sick every two weeks or so throughout my whole imprisonment because the conditions were so poor. On this visit, I was attempting to get antibiotics. Five Al-Qaeda members with big beards and lifeless eyes came walking in towards a patient that was one of the many inmates that could be found in the nearby drug wards selling themselves for drugs. The Al-Qaeda members were all facing the death penalty for gunning down a Sunni sheikh sympathetic to the regime in Iran and had nothing to lose. They began to violently stab the man in the infirmary in front of my eyes. Once done, they made eye contact with me. I locked eyes with one man, knife in hand, and his face covered in blood. Despite the possibility of them targeting me next, I couldn't move. I was shocked. The five men quickly walked out of the infirmary, leaving the bloodied corpse lying on the ground. The benefit of killing someone while you are already on death row is that the new murder requires a new trial and conviction, which could take years. The killers were buying themselves more time by killing more inmates. That night after roll call, I laid on my bunk, still shocked at how I ended up in this madness. What the hell was I doing in an Iranian prison watching Al-Qaeda members tear apart a man with shanks?

I had been alone for so long that my arrival at Ward 350 felt like an upgrade. The novelty was beginning to wear off. Yes, I wasn't in solitary confinement anymore. I was able to wear my clothes and eat better food. The fact of the matter, though, was that even with these upgrades, I was still in prison. I started having difficulties sleeping at night. I felt guilty for the pain I knew I was causing my family, and I was ashamed that I couldn't be there for my sick father. Ward 350 was no cakewalk. There was a massive bed bug infestation, rats, and due to lack of ventilation I was constantly sick with stomach, and respiratory infections. I would frequently wake up to see bed bugs crawling over my body. At night we'd all be woken up by a prisoner screaming about a huge rat chewing into his things in search of food. We had a process in place. One of us would grab a broom stick and trap the rat against the wall, while another would clobber it over the head with whatever blunt object we had at the time. These were enormous, red eyed rats that gave us all nightmares.

On top of the daily struggles in Evin, I had gotten word that my father had a cancerous tumor in his brain. The brain tumor was discovered a few months after my arrest. He later went on to have a stroke. No matter how many times I was told that the cancerous tumor caused his stroke, I couldn't help but feel distressed that my arrest was really at fault. The guilt that what happened to me caused my father's stroke would tear me apart, and continues to hurt me to this day.

Chapter Twenty-Five:
Endure

At night, I would feel sadness, then hopelessness, then feelings of anger and rage because I could not be there for my mother and father when they needed me most. Most prisoners, especially innocent ones, would share my feeling of wanting to cut out the part of the brain that has memory and emotion to avoid not only being a prisoner to this regime but being a prisoner to their own minds — this way the body alone could do the time, like a rock - lifeless and without feeling. Prison can either make you emotionally invincible or break you to the point of no recourse. By this time, I had found out that I had been sentenced to ten years. I had to find a way not just to survive this experience but to thrive in this environment. Ten years was too long to be angry. I had to think about the impact this experience would leave on me when I survived this place.

I went through two terrible withdrawals from the pills they had fed in me Ward 209. While they are a necessity for those dealing with mental illness, they were used as a method of torture on me. When I was told I would need to be re-evaluated by medical personnel in Ward 350 to continue to receive them, I didn't bother. I was going to do my sentence on my terms. As my time in Ward 350 stretched on, I found myself again. Even though I occasionally went through emotional cycles, my confidence in being able to handle them was greater. The longer I was in prison, the less they affected me. With acceptance came peace.

The days began to pass quickly. I no longer looked to political events for hope. I no longer asked my family for updates on the work they were doing back in the United States to try to gain my release. I decided that I was going to use this opportunity to grow. I had a full schedule every day. I had access to books and spent a great amount of time reading and learning about subjects that piqued my curiosity. I exercised. I helped other prisoners by teaching exercises and calisthenics and giving English lessons. I would have deep conversations about politics with political detainees. I regularly discussed physics and space with a brilliant physicist who had been imprisoned on charges of cooperating with the CIA. I discussed foreign policy and international relations with another professor who had worked in Iran's National Security Council. Ward 350 had lived up to its nickname of Evin University.

My faith in God had increased 100-fold, and I felt closer to him than at any other time in my life. The religious verses that speak of blessings in disguise were particularly special to me. I did wonder if this thinking was a coping mechanism, but with distance and hindsight, I know my belief was true. Reaching this state of mental resilience in prison would allow me to hit the ground running whenever I was released and found myself back in the free world. My hope shifted from just getting home to what I would do post-release. I began to consider my future in a way I had taken for granted before I found myself imprisoned in Iran. I imagined the day that I would come home to my family stronger and wiser than I was when I had last said goodbye. I hoped the joy that we would feel that day would make up for some of the pain they had endured during my long absence.

This growth is how I would rebel against my captors. The MOIS had set up surveillance cameras in Ward 350 that could be viewed by our interrogators live. When they watched me, I wanted them to see me on camera working out, reading, and unbroken by the evil they had imposed upon me. Being an American and a Marine inferred a responsibility in me to represent something bigger than myself with how I conducted myself in Ward 350. Since my case had been publicized so much on Iranian state television, these were details about my life that my fellow inmates knew before I took my first step into the ward. Breaking down in prison wouldn't just hurt me, but the reputation of America and our military. I was in prison with many people who had been given harsh sentences – decades in prison or execution – for helping the American government. I especially felt their eyes watching me for confirmation that it had all been worth it.

Iranian state media began promoting the JCPOA Nuclear Deal. It was an effort to change public opinion in support of the deal. The Supreme Leader, Ayatollah Ali Khamenei, signaled this the most when he publicly stated that Iran needed to show heroic flexibility. Some of the prisoners would laugh hysterically and say that the Supreme Leader was bluffing. How could he go from daily chants of "Death to America!" for 40 years to a call for "heroic flexibility"? On the other hand, words of peace and de-escalation were good to hear, especially to someone like me who had witnessed the horrors of combat. The political detainees were emphatic that you should never trust a mullah, though, and that Khamenei just wanted to get sanctions off so he could go back to more nefarious plans.

One example of this two-faced diplomacy was the arrest of Washington Post reporter Jason Rezaian. Leading up to the days of the public announcement of his arrest by Iranian State TV, they had used propaganda to hype his arrest. Prisoners of Ward 350 would see daily news bulletins that big news was coming. After sufficiently building up the hype around the story, Iranian media finally broke the news. "Iran's brilliant security services arrest dangerous CIA spy" We all anxiously awaited more details or a picture, and one appeared. It was the baby-faced Jason Rezaian. The prison Ward 350 burst into laughter. Iranian State Media had lost any credibility.

"This is the guy!" a cellmate said. "Ooooh, scary!" another said.

It was comical that this was their biggest story at a time when US sanctions on Iran were crushing its economy, poverty was at a high, and drug addiction was rampant. The political detainees pointed to the media story and used it as proof of their opposition to Iran's supposed goodwill in negotiations. A common saying among prisoners was, "The Mullahs will lead you to the water and bring you back thirsty." Many of their suspicions may have been confirmed even before the JCPOA when Iran detained US Navy sailors and paraded them at gunpoint on television. Despite all the signs of my potential release, I kept my head down and continued to do my time so my time wouldn't do me.

Chapter Twenty-Six:

Desperation

"Amir Hekmati to the front. You have a medical appointment."

I did not know about any pending medical appointment, nor had I requested to see any doctor. My cellmates looked at me. Some with excitement in my eyes as they suspected I was going to be released, some with worry, others with resentment that freedom may come to me and not them. I whispered to Majid that if I didn't come back, I needed him to get word to my family and that he could have whatever belongings I left behind. I grabbed my sandals and headed to the front door, where a guard was waiting with a document in his hand. Tight-lipped, he wouldn't tell me where we were going. We had walked a while when my heart dropped. I remembered this walk from years ago. We were headed back to Ward 209. I was going back to solitary. We entered the gate to Ward 209, and I was passed off to the plain-clothed MOI guards. They handed me the dreaded blindfold and instructed me to put it on.

"Mr. Amir, how are you?" a familiar voice asked, "Why do you think they brought you here?"

"I think the Ministry of Intelligence and Haji are ashamed of the mistake they made in imprisoning me and want to show how sorry they are by letting me go."

One of the guards took my quip especially personal and grabbed my arm, and swiftly escorted me to a solitary confinement cell. I didn't fight him. I simply walked in the cell, laid down, and fell asleep. Bruce Lee once said, "You must be shapeless, formless, like water. When you pour water in a cup, it becomes the cup. When you pour water in a bottle, it becomes the bottle. When you pour water in a teapot, it becomes the teapot. Water can drip, and it can crash. Become like water, my friend." I was water.

I was woken up with a bang on the door. The guard yelled for me to put my blindfold on and step out. I was walked to a building where one of the prosecutors in my case was waiting inside a nice office. Chocolates and flowers had been put on the table in front of me.

"How are you doing, Amir?" he asked in a friendly tone. I didn't answer.

"You have been here a long time, Amir. We are considering pardoning you. We need you to apologize on camera for being a spy before we can do that, though. Ok?"

I looked at him, stared at the camera, and glanced at the chocolates. My blood began to boil. They were trying to create a propaganda video and make it look as if my time being beaten, tortured, and abused didn't happen at all, and I was staying in some luxurious suite inside Evin Prison with chocolates and flowers. In the back of my mind, I couldn't help but rage and my blood began to boil. But... what if they really meant it? No, no, I had to shake this thought out of my head. In a letter I smuggled from prison to then-Secretary of State John Kerry and made public, I made it clear that I didn't want to be considered for a prisoner swap. I didn't want to be released for any reason other than an admission of my innocence by the Iranians that had put me here.

I was strong. If I refuse and the prosecutor sent me back to prison, I would be fine. I thought about my freedom. I hated that I had been tricked into making the first propaganda video. I didn't want to live the rest of my life with a video absolving Iran of everything they did to me while I was imprisoned there and pretend that the torment, torture, and abuse did not happen.

"I'll say on the video what I've been telling you all along, Mr. Prosecutor. You imprisoned me even though you knew I was innocent, so shame on you. You should go on camera and ask for my forgiveness, and not the other way around."

The room went quiet. I waited for the prosecutor to call the guards in and tell them to take me away. Instead, he looked stunned. He realized that their threats and trickery no longer had any power over me.

"You may go," he said in a quiet voice.

I began to prepare myself for a night in solitary confinement. To my surprise, we were not heading back to Ward 209. We were not heading back to Ward 350. I was taken to a parking lot with several cars waiting.

Chapter Twenty-Seven:
Departure

Guards approached from different directions. Each set of guards had another prisoner with them: The Christian pastor Saeed Abedini, Washington Post reporter Jason Rezaian, and two other Americans I didn't know. I was escorted into a vehicle, and a convey was formed. We sped through heavy traffic towards Mehrabad airport. I wondered if the prosecutor had tried to solicit recorded apologies in exchange for freedom from the other Americans. I was proud that I had stood my ground.

We arrived at what appeared to be a special VIP room in Mehrabad Airport. Several MOIS guards hovered around the room while we impatiently waited to find out what would happen next. Little did we know that it would be hours before we would be allowed to leave. Meal carts arrived and placed in front of us. After years of the finest meals Evin Prison had to offer, this was the most amazing dinner spread I had seen in my life. I couldn't wait to dig in. The door opened, and several cameramen stumbled in. They weren't offering us this meal in good faith. It was a photo opportunity. I remembered the words of the political detainees: The Mullahs will lead you to water and bring you back thirsty.

Saeed and I looked at one another. We had both spent enough time under the Iranian's "care" to subject ourselves to this humiliation. We would not be pawns in their propaganda game. As the cameraman was setting up, Saeed and I leapt up and ran into the bathroom and shut the door. We yelled at the cameraman to take his camera and to break it over his damn head!

After the cameraman left, we stepped out. I told the MOIS guards in the room to take their food and dump it on their heads.

They looked at me like they wanted to kill me, and if this were Ward 209, bad things would happen to me. I know because these men were made from the same cloth as those men that told me my family had died in a car accident, used their batons to communicate with me when they were not happy, and stole valuable time with my father away from me. They all answered to the same god, and that god's name was power. I knew they had orders to deliver us to freedom and nothing else. They wouldn't risk anything by acting on their hate. After they realized that we were not going to be active participants in this last-ditch photo opportunity, they escorted us to meet the Swiss Ambassador in an airport lounge.

"You're the first official I've seen that wasn't Iranian. It is so good to meet you," I said to Swiss Ambassador Haas, a towering figure with a big smile. He greeted each of us with a handshake and told us how hard they worked to get us there and how happy he was that we were going home. We were escorted on the runway where the Swiss Ambassadors luxury jet was waiting. We were greeted by the flight attendants who directed us to the luxury seats inside the plane. Attendants immediately took orders with the menu consisting of champagne, chocolates, and veal.

The cabin door shut, and preparations were underway for takeoff. We looked out the window and could see MOIS personnel and Swiss officials on the runway making frantic calls. Other MOIS agents quickly entered the plane to take photos. We could tell the communications were intense, and negotiations were underway. After a day of delay, the plane engine revved and we were wheels up. I looked for Evin Prison, but we were too far. I was now that bird flying up above the prison yard I dreamed for years to be. The parts of myself I closed off so I could survive and do my time was slowly coming back to me. For the first time since I surprised my grandmother in her home four and a half years ago, I felt joy.

I anxiously watched the digital map inside the plane's cabin for the moment we left Iranian airspace and were no longer within reach of the evil regime below. Once we crossed out of Iran, the plane erupted in cheers, and we celebrated our freedom with one another. Flight attendants shared in the joy by popping a bottle of champagne. I stared at the clouds from the window of the plane. This was real. This is what it meant to be free. Finally.

Chapter Twenty-Eight:
Family, Again

We were overlooking Lake Geneva as we descended upon the Swiss airport. We could see reporters in the distance, and Brett McGurk, the Presidential Envoy on ISIS and lead negotiator for our release, was outside the plane to greet us. We were ushered onto another plane where the Deputy Secretary of State, Antony Blinken, and Special Envoy for Iranian Affairs Jennifer Farrar were aboard and ready to greet us. Jennifer was the intermediary between the US government and the Swiss Embassy in Tehran.

After a short flight, we arrived at Landstuhl Airbase. We had a brief medical examination and were interviewed by officials. They were especially interested in knowing if we had heard anything about Robert Levinson while we were in prison in Iran. After the debriefing, we were released to our families anxiously awaiting our arrival. Waiting for me was my big sister Sarah, who represented my family and campaigned hard for my release, my brother-in-law, Ramy, my twin sister, Leila, and Congressman Kildee of Michigan's 5th District. Representative Kildee and his team worked doggedly with my family for my release. He remained in constant contact with President Obama and Iranian officials to make sure that I wasn't forgotten and spoke about my imprisonment many times on the House floor. I'm confident that were it not for Representative Kildee's support, I would have served all ten years of my sentence.

Being reunited with my family was like being able to breathe again. On January 16, 2016, I was reborn.

Eager to leave Landstuhl Airbase with my family, we first had to pass a crowd of reporters eagerly awaiting to interview us. I was anxious for the chance to finally have a voice. I knew that many Americans offered support and prayer for my family and me during one of the lowest points in our lives and I wanted to thank them for their love, care, and kindness. I used the opportunity to thank President Obama and members of Congress, specifically Representative Kildee, and the people from my hometown of Flint, Michigan. I also wanted to thank my fellow Marines. I would later learn that a group of Marines – those I knew and those I didn't - had gone on hunger strike with me and did their best to raise awareness about my imprisonment and lobby for my release.

Our release was bigger than securing the freedom of a few Americans. Our release brought Americans together and set an example for people all over the world for what a government is supposed to be and the efforts it should go through for its citizens. The campaign to secure our freedom touched the hearts of the political prisoners inside the Iranian prison who sacrificed their lives for their beliefs. I remembered watching videos in prison on Iranian state TV showing then-Secretary of State John Kerry calling for our release and other prisoners being astonished at how such a powerful government rallied behind a handful of its citizens in a foreign prison a world away.

Once we landed in New York's JFK, my family and I were escorted from the plane by DHS agents to a private jet loaned to us for the special occasion by Phil Hagermann, a wealthy Michigan businessman. The closer we came to Michigan, the more I was able to relax. I was going home. We landed at Flint's Bishop Airport and were greeted by hundreds of Flint residents who were waiting in the Michigan winter to welcome me home. I walked by hundreds of residents and gave as many handshakes and hugs as I could. I told the waiting reporters how much I loved and respected the people of Flint, and I meant it. No matter where I go in the world, Flint will always be close to my heart.

And then it was time to reunite with the person I missed the most, my mother. As she wrapped her arms around me, I thanked God that we were a family again.

EPILOGUE:

For 40 years the US and Iran have been engaged in a covert war with many people like myself caught in the middle. At the moment of this writing Americans are being held in Iranian prisons as this war continues. I hope to bring attention to their plight, and give the reader an understanding of the devastating impact this will have on them, and their families. The US and Iran despite all the rhetoric have no desire to engage in direct confrontation, and have chosen war by proxy, that has claimed many victims. The USA imposing crippling sanctions that affect the people of Iran, and Iran by taking innocent people hostage, and wreaking chaos in neighboring countries like Iraq, Syria, and Lebanon. Protests in Iraq show an entire population held captive in a proxy war between the USA, and Iran. Iraqi youth wanting relations with the USA, and a modern country on one side, while Iranian backed militias and power centers aligned with the Islamic Republic, and it's so called theocracy on the other. For those caught in the crossfire, there is no clear, or easy solution.

For ordinary Iranians whose only fault was to be born in a country with a government hostile to the United States, the choices are limited. Join the Iranian government in its hostility for which the majority of ordinary Iranians refuse, oppose the Iranian government and risk prison or worse, or simply drudge along enduring the imposed hardships caused by the fallout. As Iranian Americans the choice is to say goodbye to your heritage and relatives in Iran, or risk travel to a country willing to use you as a political pawn. Trapped in this war what kept me alive, and sane was faith, the support of my family, and rationalizing my fate in a way I could accept.

As with any traumatic event, the first step is to stabilize, find calm, and acclimatize to the trauma. Once I was able to normalize what was happening to me, I had to preserve my physical, and mental health to allow normalization to take effect. I did this by finding my props such as a daily routine, exercise, and above all faith in God and love for family. For me, I was unable to find enough motivation in self preservation to survive this ordeal. I needed external reasons, and found them in the want to see my family again, and ease their pain, not mine. I didn't want them to see me destroyed emotionally in a filthy Iranian prison far from home. My faith taught me that we all would deal with calamity in this life, that suicide would be met with eternal damnation, and that self destruction was easy, anyone could do it. Whenever I thought about the man I would become having survived this ordeal knowing I never gave in I would get a little uplift to carry me through the day. We all need to have that curiosity when dealing with calamity.

When we are in a horrific situation, and all appears lost, we can easily succumb and fall apart. However, what if we made it through? That triumph would be ingrained in our soul, and go to the graves with us, something that could never be taken from me, despite all that was being stolen from me in Evin prison. I realized that when I had reached the point where I felt I could go no longer, and all was gone, I had only yet reached the very beginning of what I was capable of. I would go on to endure 4 more years, when at the time I didn't believe I would survive another day. This belief system was not infallible. I would relapse often, and fall into a dark place mentally. To overcome this, I needed to create outcomes in my mind that didn't fall within the limited time allowed in this life. Many of us can be dealt blows so severe that recovering from them fully would be impossible in a lifetime. There just simply isn't enough years in one's life to fully recover from 10, 20, 30 years in prison, a paralyzing accident, a major illness, the loss of a child, and so on. When we are confined to see our problems within the context of one's lifetime they can be impossible to overcome. It helped immensely to begin to look outside of this lifetime, and into the afterlife. In creating this mental space I could relieve myself to a degree the undeniable devastation this ordeal had caused me, and the vision I had for my life. This life was fleeting, a short drop in the proverbial bucket of history spanning billions of years.

Traumatic events of this magnitude cannot be dealt with solely based on fact, or science. The human mind requires a belief in something extraterrestrial. Yes you may not fully recover from that event, yes you may never achieve the dreams you held so dearly now that the event happened, but this world was only a stop on a much larger journey. The belief in something greater than this world, and life was crucial in my survival, and in dealing with the continued hardships that linger even to this day. I will never get back what I lost, but try to focus on what I gained, and the futility of this world. Had I lived a perfect life, and achieved everything on my endless wishlist, it would still end abruptly from old age, or one of thousands of other afflictions we face in life. This sort of comparative thinking helped me countless times. I was in prison, but I was alive. I would lose 10 years, but I would gain patience, and strength. I was in prison, but on the news I read about a man free as a bird, but paralyzed from a car accident. There was always a comparison to give my trauma context, and help me frame the situation in my mind in a way that I could draw on gratitude instead of misery, depression, or anger. Prison gave me a glimpse into my soul, and what would remain once my life ended. There is a beauty in being imprisoned, and the time spent contemplating one's self. You begin to know your soul like a free man never would. I felt that life was about building your eternal soul, not about achieving worldly greatness, but soul greatness. I was on this earth to build my soul into an eternal record of sorts.

The "record" of oneself that will carry with you into the next life. In us is an innate understanding of right, and wrong that prison illuminates for those who seek to improve themselves, and gain that insight. Your deeds, actions, and the way we feel about our own soul would be magnified in my psyche while confined in those walls. The soul would be all that would remain, and would serve as the true judge of success in this fleeting life. Amir Hekmati was not a sum of my worldly achievements, my wealth, or how others viewed me. I was not a sum of how much pain I avoided in this life, and how much pleasure, and fun I had. I was not a bag of skin, and bones that would rot, and turn to dirt one day. I was a bundle of memories that my soul was collecting, and compiling into a final record that would carry with me into the next world. The beauty of prison was how in touch I became with this record of one's self. Prison was a magnifying glass into one's soul. If your heart and soul was that of a good person, prison would fill your heart with more light, and strengthen your faith. If there was darkness in your heart, prison would corrupt your soul even more. Some of the inmates in Evin had eye pupils that seemed to turn blacker and blacker the longer they stayed in. In prison you are the living dead, and you could begin to see how the other prisoners' souls would appear in the afterlife. Those who were in prison for the wrong reasons like protesting against corruption, or their spiritual beliefs only seemed to grow stronger, and find a certain spiritual invincibility. Their faces would fill with light, and passing them gave me a sort of calm. My new motivation was to cultivate that connectedness to my soul, and do everything possible to use my time in this life to transfer to myself the best record possible into the next life. The immediate challenge in front of me was to overcome the imposed hardship of this prison. My soul would bear witness for me in the next world of how I maintained my faith, and never wavered under those pressures. With this mindset, the pain, and angst over the loss of my time, and freedoms to prison were forgotten.

Whether this was just a coping mechanism, or a new discovery about myself is debatable, but I'm inclined to believe the latter. Regardless, my new belief system helped me immensely in getting through the incredible pain, and hardship. I was able to let go of what I would stand to lose from this unjust imprisonment, and began to see this as an opportunity. If the goal of this life was to build your soul to support you in the next life, then this was the ultimate building ground to do just that.

What good would it be for me to be free, and go about this life lost chasing worldly goals that can never be fully achieved, and have no knowledge of my own soul? I can say with the utmost conviction that my soul is not the same as the one I had when I entered Evin on that terrifying day in 2011. I re-entered the world with an awareness of self I would never have achieved without that horrific experience. Some say that we all grieve differently, and handle affliction in different ways. I hope to share this experience, and my deepest thoughts to help those being afflicted in the same ways. I hope this writing has given you some useful perspective, and may you have the strength and patience to survive the hardships that we all will inevitably face.

Made in the USA
Monee, IL
26 May 2020